T2-CSE-146

Parent and Teenager/Living & Loving

Parent and Teenager Living & Loving

EVELYN MILLIS DUVALL

BROADMAN PRESS
NASHVILLE, TENNESSEE

Dewey Decimal Classification: 301.427
Subject Headings: FAMILY/PARENT AND CHILD/ADOLESCENCE
Library of Congress Catalog Card Number: 75-18005
Printed in the United States of America

CONTENTS

1
No One Like a Teen!

A child is a child. An adult is a grown-up. But a teenager is like neither, and both. No longer a child, at least much of the time. Not yet an adult in anyone's eyes. A teenage youngster lives in a never-never land he has not known before and may never know again. How he got there he is not quite sure. What is expected of him is often uncertain. Where he is going is the question that preoccupies him most of all. Who he is and what he is going to do about himself is an all-pervasive puzzle.

One thing is sure—a teen is not his parents. He does not look like either of them in every respect. He does not act like them in many ways. He does not think like them. His judgment is not theirs. His dreams and hopes and ambitions are his own. His feelings are neither as reliable nor as stable as those of his parents. He or she is himself or herself—whatever that means.

Each Is Unique

A teenager, boy or girl, is like no other person he or she has ever known. He was born a unique individual with his own built-in program for development. He grew through childhood in his own special way. He entered adolescence according to his own personal timetable. He goes through the teen years at his own rate. He or she today is the individual once known as a little boy or girl. But what a difference now that childish ways are being cast off! The older he grows the more like himself he becomes. All his strengths and weaknesses, **7** all his assets and liabilities, all his sweetness and his disagreeableness are him—as he is today.

No two are alike in the family. Mothers often report that no two of their children are like one another. One is active and into everything, another is quiet and reserved. One is easy to talk with, another tends to be uncommunicative. One can be disciplined with a look, another requires more stringent methods. Studies find that no two children come into the same family. The first one is the only child for awhile and becomes the parents' first assistant. The second arrives and, finding the responsible role filled, goes in another direction—often into social life in the neighborhood. Subsequent children each find their own special place in the family, according to their strengths, weaknesses, and position in the family.

Children in the family have to be different. Each needs to feel that he or she is special and like none other. Parents are wise to encourage each of their children and teenagers to find themselves in the particular ways that make sense to them. This is what teenagers mean when they insist upon doing "their own thing." They do not relish having to act like, feel like, and respond like a brother or sister whom their parents hold up as a model. Comparing one child with another is a poor policy and often boomerangs in unhappy ways.

Parents are puzzled about their teenagers, oftentimes. They are baffled by adolescents' changing moods and erratic behavior. They are not quite sure what is happening to these growing-up children of theirs, whom once they felt they knew so well. They wonder what roles they should be playing as mothers and fathers of teenagers. What should they tell them? What should they do? They wonder why they as parents have so many different feelings about their own teenage children. Sometimes they admire and are proud of them. Sometimes parents wonder what on earth has gotten into the children to make them act as they do. At times parents thoroughly enjoy their teenage sons and daughters, and at other times they find their behavior, appearance, friends, and activities hard to accept.

Adults generally blow hot and cold about teenage youth. Attitudes in school, church, and community range widely from enthusiastic approval of teenagers to intensely critical attacks upon them. The daily paper reflects the ambivalent feelings about teenagers abroad in the area. Headlines recount in detail the escapades, accidents, vandalism, sex activities, drug episodes, and other "bad news" that teenagers generate. Other stories in newspapers cite youth for their many accomplishments and capabilities. Few adults are calmly accepting of teenagers. Their own feelings are too intense to allow it.

Teens Are Children Older Grown

Persistence of personality is as true of teenagers as it is of all other people. Each individual early develops his own patterns of behaving, feeling, relating, and responding to a wide variety of situations and persons. These reflect what the individual is genetically—all his or her inherited characteristics and tendencies. They result from the person's early experiences of success and failure, love or neglect, good and not so good. The composite of inherited and learned qualities becomes the recognizable personality each individual is. All other experiences are assimilated or rejected by this basic personality that has been there all along.

Each is what he has always been, plus what he or she is going through currently. As a teenager, a youngster is struggling to become a mature human being. This puts added burdens and responsibilities on him and his parents. It also brings its own incentives in the form of the privileges of being more mature. The motivation for maturing is intense at times, causing the teenager to struggle against his own childish ways as well as away from his parents who knew him when he was "just a child." But essentially, each is the same person he or she has always been, now going through a new stage of development into which he brings his characteristic ways of responding and relating.

Teen adjustments are built upon earlier ones. Children who have been happy and successful as youngsters tend to bring to their adolescence the expectation of continued happiness and success. Unhappy, poorly adjusted children experience greater difficulties during their teen years, when their problems are even more severe than they were in earlier years. An illustration is found in the child with reading disabilities. His early struggle to keep up with his classmates and measure up to his parents' expectations have given him a sense of failure. He enters junior and senior high school not as well equipped as his fellow students for the more difficult assignments of secondary school. So, his poor adjustment continues, not because he is now a teenager, but essentially because of the continuation of the dyslexia that has always been a burden to him.

Parent-teen relationships continue those established during childhood. A mother who has had a hard time letting her children go is apt to find releasing them as teenagers even harder. Now that they are big enough to resist her possessiveness more strenuously, she is threatened and unsure of herself and of them. A father who has been too busy to relate to his sons and daughters when they were young now experiences an added sense of distance from them as teenagers. One such man put it clearly when he said, "I feel as though I were living with a couple of strangers now that my two kids are teenagers." Actually they always were strangers—only he did not know it.

The persistence of relationships over time has its advantages, too. Parents who have always been able to communicate well with their children find that the teen years add a new depth and dimension to their relationships with their teenagers. These older sons and daughters level with them in all candor in what can be an exhilarating experience for members of both generations. Jennie Lou put it well when she said: "My folks are simply super. There is not anything I can't discuss with them. They know me so well that I feel utterly safe with them, even when I've made a mess of things. So I talk over what I loused up, and we go on from there. They don't say, 'Why didn't you do it right to begin with?' They know I do the best I can, under the circumstances. With their confidence, I somehow get strong enough to surmount almost anything."

Parents can find comfort in the knowledge that the relationships they have established with their youngsters as children tend to carry on into the teen years. These relationships will naturally become more mature, as the children grow. But their basic nature remains. Teenagers are not some strangely difficult race dropped into the family from some distant planet; they are the same familiar people who have lived there throughout their lives. Knowing oneself and one's children is a great protection from the scary generalizations that surround teenagers today.

The Teens—Terrible Years?

Many parents dread the teen years even before their children reach them. Teenagers are generally felt to be so hard to control and so difficult to live with that many a mother and father expect to be hard put to live with their teenage children.

Parents are almost expected to be critical of their teens. When the author asked one well-known pair of parents of three teenagers what they would suggest that would help in writing this book, they replied almost in unison, "Take them off our hands for a while." Their attitude was that they had had almost more than they could stand with their teenage daughter and her two younger brothers in their early teens. Pressed for details of parents' problems with teenagers, these usually calm parents gave heated responses peppered with such criticisms as "insolent," "brash," "irresponsible," "disrespectful," "sulky," "difficult to reach," and "mean to one another and to us."

Some parents say that they are afraid for their teenagers. There are so many hazards that beset young people in the modern community that parents fear teenagers will be irreparably hurt. They read the scary headlines about jams that teenagers get into and tremble with anxiety that their own youngsters may not escape them.

It seems as though parents sometimes are afraid of their teenage children. These modern adolescents seem so big, so bold, so sophisticated, so young, so smart, and so sure that they cow their parents into submission. The familiar taunts: "You just don't understand." "No one does it that way anymore." "Times have changed since you were young." "This is my life, and I'll do with it as I please." "Cool it, folks, I know what I'm doing." These are enough to send all but the most secure parent scuttling back to adult circles where people are at least courteous to one another. Well, most of the time, anyway!

Do they have to be so messy? This is frequently heard wherever two or more mothers are discussing their teenagers. The accounts range from dirty clothes strewn about the house, to unkempt rooms, and on to sloppy grooming and attire of young people who once took pride in keeping themselves and their possessions attractive. The matter of hair length and cleanliness becomes an issue beyond its importance in many a family. One mother finds her son's hair so repulsive, she can't stand the sight of him before breakfast. So she puts his food on the table for him and then takes her mug of coffee upstairs until he has left for school. This is hardly the way to bridge the generation gap, but it does illustrate the intensity of feeling that some teenagers generate in their parents.

"Disrespect I will not tolerate," says one red-faced father, recounting a recent altercation between his son and himself. The father says his boy was brought up to "respect his elders" and not to talk back to his mother and father. Now that he is a teenager, the boy ridicules their ideas, refuses to reply to their questions, and is openly insulting to them both. The father is almost beyond his patience in trying to insist that his son give proper respect to his parents. These parents find that what used to work in controlling their son no longer is

effective, so they throw up their hands in dismay and shout themselves hoarse—all to no avail.

"It's not easy being teenagers," say youngsters themselves. They agree that the teen years are terrible for them, too, in many ways. They no longer have the comforts and pleasures of childhood. They miss the cuddling and encouragement they knew as children. A girl is too big to sit on her father's lap and be comforted as she once was. A boy now feels too grown up to confide in his parents about the problems or even the successes he is having. Both boys and girls are afraid of being lectured when they wonder about what is right or wrong these days, so they keep their questions to themselves in many families. They hesitate even to recount the goings on among other teenagers, for fear their parents will conclude that they, too, are headed for trouble.

"I'm so unpredictable these days," is a recurrent experience of boys and girls in the teen years. One girl goes on to elaborate her observation about herself. "One day I feel wonderful, in love with the whole world, and everyone in it. The next day, for no reason at all that I can see, I'm so disagreeable I can hardly stand myself. I snarl at my brothers and sisters, snap at my mother, and avoid my father entirely." Such shifting moods are baffling. They account for many of the upsets in the lives of young people and those who live with them.

Even the physical aspect of life is uncertain during the early teen years. A youngster going through a period of rapid growth is apt to be clumsy. His arms and legs are longer than they used to be. His feet are bigger, and his coordination has not kept up with the growth of his long bones. So he bumps into things, spills things at the table, and actually is going through an awkward stage that will last until he has attained some stability of size and performance. This will all come in time, but meanwhile it is not easy to live with—as a teenager or as those who care about him or her.

Socially the teen years are experimental. Teenagers ache to belong and to be accepted as attractive, likable human beings.

Friends their own age are terribly important to them now when they need the support of their own generation. Sometimes they try too hard to get in with the teenagers they most admire and are rebuffed. More often, they are too shy and uncertain of themselves to go out to others in the friendly ways that are effective. So they try off-beat ways to attract attention or give too much of themselves too soon in the hope of being accepted. It takes years to find oneself among others of both sexes, all ages, and social sets. In the meantime, each one learns by experience, by trying out what works and what does not. Experience often is painful. Experiments fail as well as succeed. So the teen years are uncertain—for parents and for teenagers.

Teenagers Are Terrific

Teenagers can be terrific human beings. They can bring proud tears to the eyes of their parents when they carry through some difficult responsibility with courageous success. They get recognition at church or school for some project well done, and their family shares their pleasure. They give themselves to some worthy project with such intensity that the whole family gets caught up in it. Gloria got so involved in her girls' club recycling drive that even her kid brother was out after school helping collect aluminum cans and newspapers. Bert threw himself into a history project with such enthusiasm that his whole family traveled to the state capitol to look up some elusive data with him. The Smith kids started a clean-up project in their neighborhood park that got them cited by the chamber of commerce. Everywhere all across the country teenagers are demonstrating what wonderful persons they can be.

Talents blossom in ways that amaze and delight their parents during the teen years. Sylvia, who so long resisted music lessons as a youngster, now serves as assistant church organist. Joe, whose tendency to stutter as a boy worried him and his family, now has the lead in his school play. Joyce, who nursed hurt kittens and puppies as a little girl, now serves faithfully as a candy striper in the hospital nearby. Butch, always an athlete, now has a scholarship to the university of his choice, and that pleases his father quite as much as does his son's good grades.

Responsibilities are carried in the teen years that impress all who live with teenagers. Intellectual interests bring exciting questions to the fore, so that there is never a dull moment with teenagers in many a home. Social life widens both personal and family horizons, as Mother drives a carload of teenagers to an area meet, or Father volunteers to teach his son's class at the YMCA.

Ability to withstand temptation in the modern community is remarkable. So outstanding that many an anxious parent wonders if it can last. How long can a youngster stand up against pressures to smoke, to drink, to drive like crazy, or to act out sexually the torments of the teen years? How much help do young people need in order to remain strong and "good" these days?

It's harder to be good now than it was when parents and grandparents were young. Then the pressures were toward decent, responsible behavior. Things were good or bad, and most people agreed on which was which. Opportunities to get into trouble were present but not with the commercial appeal that hawks them today. Fewer teenagers expected to drive their own cars as soon as they were old enough to be licensed drivers. Drugs were not so readily available. Alcoholic beverages were served only in the most "sophisticated" homes. "Getting into trouble" was a blot on a girl's reputation, and "tangling with the police" was not something of which a boy was proud.

Supervision in home, school, and community was more rigid and consistent in former generations than it tends to be today. Families knew where their young people were more often than is possible nowadays. Neighbors and friends kept an eye on other people's children and served *in loco parentis* in ways unheard of today.

"Being a virgin when I married was no particular credit to me," says Grandma Jones. She goes on to regale her grandchildren with how closely chaperoned she was as a girl. How cleverly Mother stepped onto the porch at just the right moment when she and her "best beau" were courting. Whether it was to bring refreshing lemonade or homemade ice cream, the timing was perfect. She never got so far away from home with her date that some neighbor or family friend did not greet her by name, ask to meet her boyfriend, and to wish the couple well. She said she rarely felt restricted but surely never knew the freedom and the anonymity that young people have today.

Grandma Jones's great-granddaughter is a stranger ten minutes from her own front door. So many new people have moved into the neighborhood since her family settled there that they do not know her or what to expect of her. She herself has moved from one place to another so much that she has no teachers who knew her as a youngster. Even her pastor is new to her, and she to him. She goes to a big high school with thousands of other students who crowd the corridors, jam the stairs, and meet in huge classes where few are known as individuals with families, and backgrounds, and ideals to be recognized and respected.

"Who will know?" is the oft-repeated phrase accompanying some daredevil challenge. In the old days most of the persons important to a youngster would know, and soon. Now few who know or care are apt to be aware of what is going on— whatever it is. When a teenager is a number on an IBM card at school, and "just another kid in jeans" in town, he or she can feel that few know or care what goes on in his life.

A teenager has to be sure of himself in order to find his way amid the confusions and contradictions of today's world. He or she is no longer protected from danger during the growing years. Parents cannot go with their young people. They cannot make their decisions for them. They must stand by and trust their teenagers to carry into action the ideals and values taught them thus far. This is not easy for the teenager. Nor is it easy for those who love and live with him. That so many teens are such fine persons is a credit not only to them, but to their parents as well.

Parents Are Something Else!

George has a special way of expressing admiration. He grins at those whom he commends as he says, "You are really something else!" It doesn't make much sense put into cold print like this. But when George says it, you glow to the tips of your toes. Why? Because each of us likes to be thought unique, different, special, "something else." Parents of today's teens are truly something else in the finest sense.

Parents come through the fire of public and private criticism without wilting. They stand by their youngsters with courage and faith even when they themselves are not sure how an episode is going to turn out. They love their youngsters enough to give them the guidance they need when they need it. They do all this with humility that belies their courage.

The Johnsons right now are standing firm against their attractive sixteen-year-old daughter's insistence that she be allowed to thumb a ride to school. She feels that she is too big now to ride her bike to school as she has for years. It is too far to walk, and there is no bus that comes close enough to help. So, her proposed solution is to hitchhike, a proposal that her parents have discussed at length with her. They feel that thumbing a ride to school is far too hazardous to consider. Without unduly frightening their daughter, they are aware of the number of cases of molestation, rape, and worse that are reported regularly in their local paper. They realize that for a winsome sixteen-year-old girl to thumb rides from strangers is to ask for trouble. So they quietly and firmly insist that she under no circumstances accept rides in others' automobiles. In response to her tears and pleas, they reaffirm their faith in her. They assure her they trust her, but that the situation she is considering is dangerous. They stand united as parents in caring enough for their teenage daughter to safeguard her from unnecessary danger.

Can parents win such a confrontation? It was not until Mrs. Johnson overheard her daughter telling her best friend, "My parents won't let me thumb rides," that she realized that their parental firmness was effective. The daughter's tone of voice conveyed pride in her parents' caring enough to forbid her taking hazardous chances. She accepted their ultimatum gracefully once she understood why they took the stand they did. In fact, the family solidarity improved markedly—for awhile. Parents can savor such little successes as they come along. They need not last long to be real. Life in the family goes on from one crisis to the next. Each next step is easier or harder depending on how well the previous ones have been taken.

Being parents of teenagers means juggling the many-faceted responsibilities of home, job, community, and church with the parental resources needed by active growing teenagers. It involves budgeting time for each of the children, as he or she needs it, when they are ready for it. It includes giving their teenagers the chance to live their own lives, make their own decisions, and cope with their own problems, secure in the knowledge that their parents care about what happens and are standing by them without fail. It calls for the willingness to keep on growing as adults, so that life does not revolve entirely around the children. It demands the inner strength to stand firm for principles and values worth holding on to.

Parents are not teens—"they are something else." They are the ones who provide the secure base from which young people can launch themselves into the world. They care enough to cope with each problem as it comes along with the best they have. They love their teenagers, so they live with them as fully as they can, being the persons they are. They do not expect to be perfect. But they strive to understand and to help their growing children sense what life and love are all about.

2
Little Girl No More

Before a girl and her parents are quite ready for it, the miracle of her growing up begins. Long before the teen years, most girls realize that they no longer are little girls. The preteen years between nine and twelve are those of rapid physical, emotional, and social change for most girls. It's a wise girl who understands what is happening to her. It is a fortunate girl who can discuss freely with her parents, the many "first time only" feelings she is experiencing.

Parents and Daughters—Then and Now

Time was when women in the family were embarrassed to discuss with growing girls the amazing changes that take place as a girl becomes a woman. Many a mother in former generations thrust a pamphlet on menstruation into her daughter's hands, hoping that it would help enough so that there would be no questions about it. Adult silence and reluctance to talk freely with their children was uncomfortable for them, for their children, and for the family as a whole.

Parents try to be helpful to their growing girls today. They know how important it is for a girl to get off to a good start in her experience as a woman. They remember how they felt when they were growing up. They sense how easy it is to be confused and uncomfortable about the intimate changes taking place in their daughter's body. They realize that the good relationship they built with their daughter in childhood now forms a solid base for comfortably facing her puberty and adolescence.

Reviewing the process of maturing into womanhood can be a satisfying experience for a girl and her mother. It can bring them close with the excitement of being "the women of the family," now that the daughter is approaching her new status. It opens many shadowy areas to the light of discovery and discussion that never quite explain the full mystery of life but give a new sense of importance to living together in the family.

Father is important to the preteen girl of the family. She begins to see him in a new light now that she senses that she is no longer "his little girl." She strives to please him in special ways. She begs her mother for chances to impress him with the new skills and talents she is developing. She wants to cook a meal "all by herself" and glows when her father praises what she has done. She wants his approval of the way she looks and is openly winsome in her ways with him. More than he may realize, she looks to him for the approval and guidance and direction she knows she needs. For he is her first sweetheart, whom she especially wants to please as someone very special in her life.

When Does a Girl Become a Woman?

A girl becomes a woman over a number of years. It does not happen all at once. There is no one day that marks the complete difference between girlhood and womanhood. There are clear evidences along the way which indicate that maturation is underway. These can be known and anticipated, as they are in many families. But when a girl begins to grow up and when she will emerge a full-fledged woman on her own are impossible to denote clearly. Growing up is a process, not a single occurrence or event.

Puberty comes early, as the first sign that a girl is growing out of childhood, out of her clothes, out of her little girl status. Puberty can be defined as the period of rapid growth as a girl begins to become mature. It is first evident in her increase in height and weight, known as the "growth spurt." This can be apparent as early as the fifth grade in school. Some girls at nine or ten years of age are getting to be too tall to sit in the front row of their class picture. They have begun the process of puberty that is soon to take them into adolescence.

Girls mature earlier than do boys, in the main. During the junior high school years, most of the girls are already in their puberal growth spurt, while many of the boys are still "little guys." No one knows for sure just why this is. The truth is that girls are more mature at birth than are boys, and they continue to be ahead of boys in physical growth and development all through the first dozen or more years of life. Girls outdistancing boys of their age in growing up makes for problems—for girls, for boys, and for their families in many ways. What these difficulties are, and how they can be lived with comfortably are aspects of adolescence we will be exploring more fully throughout this book.

Maturation comes at earlier ages now than it used to. Studies of the onset of puberty in many countries, as well as the United States, reveal that today's young people generally begin to develop earlier than did their parents, grandparents, and earlier generations in the same families. The reason for this is being explored by doctors and physiologists in many countries. The best guess so far involves children's nutrition today being more nearly optimum than it was for earlier generations. Better-nourished children mature earlier, generally speaking, than do the poorly-fed. Diets rich in vitamins, minerals, and body-building proteins tend to bring the young of all species to maturation earlier than less adequate diets. Animal husbandry capitalizes on this fact. Farmers with upgraded feeding programs now bring their hogs and beef to market months before it used to be possible. Young humans respond similarly to good food over the years. The big difference is that there is no ready market for fast-maturing girls and boys. One of the problems of both parents and teenagers today is the long period of adolescent dependence.

Late-maturing girls have the advantage of having a breather before the onset of puberty is upon them. The girl whose rapid growth spurt comes after that of many of the other girls her age may feel left behind. She may wonder when she too is going to mature. She may need her parents' reassurance that she will mature when it is time and that in the meantime there is nothing to worry about. Being a little girl a bit longer gives a girl a chance to see how other girls grow up and to be somewhat more ready for adolescent changes when they come to her. She usually has more time to develop her social skills before she is thrown into boy-girl affairs where knowing how to act is so important.

By the mid-teens almost all girls are well on their way to becoming women. Some start as early as nine or ten. Most enter puberty by age eleven or twelve. A few may be well into their teens before they obviously are maturing. It makes little difference whether a girl is early or late in her maturation, except in the way she and her family feel about it. It may help to know that if her mother and her grandmothers matured early, it is likely that she will, too. If she comes from late-maturing people, she probably will be slower getting her growth.

The Sequence of Puberal Changes

Girls go through much the same changes in about the same sequence whether they mature early or late. Knowing what happens next helps a girl and her family know what to expect step by step through a girl's development into womanhood. When they understand what is happening, and what comes next in the process of maturation, they can anticipate new changes before they occur. Then when the expected signs appear they will not be a cause for consternation.

Breast development comes soon after the growth spurt has begun in most girls. The flat-chested little girl notices that her breasts are beginning to grow into more feminine curves. They continue to round out over the next two or more years until they have the full shape and size that is normal for her as a woman. There is nothing a girl can or should do to slow or to speed the development of her bosom. It all takes place from the inside out, as the female hormones in her body determine.

In time most girls wear a brassiere to give their breasts support and a neat feminine contour. Some girls are so eager to wear a bra that they get "beginners' bras" even before they are needed. There is no harm in this. It is merely a sign that a girl is proud to be on the way to becoming a full-fledged woman.

Hair appears in grown-up patterns as puberty continues. The triangle of hair low on her abdomen between the top of her legs is called pubic hair. This hair gradually becomes dark and curly, as is normal in grown-ups. Underarm hair appears about the same time and may be shaved off by the girl who does not want it to show when she wears sleeveless dresses or swimsuits. Many a girl wants to shave the hair on her legs off. When a girl feels strongly about shaving her legs, she can be given a razor and her family's blessing on grooming herself as she wishes.

Womanly curves can come too soon for comfort. During puberty a girl's hips widen and her body rounds out in typically feminine ways. Some girls are embarrassed by these new lines and do what they can to hide them. They hunch over when they "feel bumpy in front." They wear loose clothes in an effort to conceal their broadening hips and busts. Other girls do everything they can to call attention to their new shapeliness with clothes that are too tight, too skimpy, and too revealing. Any of these first efforts of a girl to adapt to her new feminine shape can make for problems with her parents.

Father can get uptight over his young daughter's flaunting of her new assets. Mothers have been known to do what they can to encourage their daughters' emergence into womanhood, when it is in line with their own feelings about it. There are parents who try to delay as long as possible the time when they admit their daughter is growing up. They insist that she continue to wear the little-girl clothing that no longer looks right. The best approach is to accept gracefully the changes in a girl's appearance and work out with her the clothing and grooming that seem appropriate.

Grooming and Makeup

During puberty and adolescence, the oil glands of the skin are especially active. This accounts for many of the skin blemishes that plague the pubescent girl. Backed-up oil festers into pimples or becomes dirt-clogged in blackheads. The most effective remedy, as well as the prevention, is frequent washing with warm water and a mild soap or detergent. Girls becoming interested in their growing bodies may experiment with the cleansing creams and lotions they have watched their mothers use and have seen advertised. Avoiding rich foods, especially fats, chocolate, and too many sweets helps to keep the skin clear. Eating fresh fruits and vegetables rather than too many high-calorie snack foods serves a double purpose of maintaining healthy skin and avoiding overweight.

Cosmetic aids for the adolescent girl are of interest to both generations. The hormones that bring on maturation activate the sweat and oil glands in the skin. This means that the girl growing into womanhood now must make sure that she does not offend others with the odors of her maturing body. She bathes frequently, and daily applies either a deodorant or an antiperspirant under her arms. This protects her clothing and assures her of "being nice to be near."

Untended hair becomes stringy as oil, sweat, and dirt accumulate in it, especially now when the glands of the skin are so active. This is one reason why so many girls make such a point of shampooing and fussing with their hair during the preteen and teen years. Keeping the hair clean with a mild shampoo is the first step to healthy hair care. How the girl wears her hair reflects the hair styles other girls she admires are following. A girl's ideas about how she likes her hair may not conform to what her parents find pleasing. Now is the time for parents to relax and realize that their daughter has to find her own way of presenting herself. This requires time for her, and patience on her parents' part. It usually is not worth a family fuss.

Nail polish and care become rituals for many a young woman-in-the-making. A year or two earlier it appeared to be too much trouble to keep her hands and feet clean. Now she is preoccupied with their care. She files and scrubs her nails, pushes back the cuticles, and tries a variety of colors on her finger and toe nails. This is all part of learning how to act as a woman and need not upset her parents.

Lipstick—now or later? A girl usually wants to wear lipstick before her parents (especially her father) feel she is old enough for such a badge of maturity. Mother may be helpful in finding pleasant soft shades of lipstick that are not objectionable. But a mother should be prepared for her daughter's resistance to wearing "baby stuff" when what she had in mind was something far more mature. Usually far more is made of such minor rebellions in the family than they merit. In time, every girl learns what is right for her. Until then, parents help most by standing by with love and trust in her ultimate judgment.

Eye makeup today is more widely accepted than it was in earlier generations. A modern girl begins early to experiment with eyeshadow, eyeliner, mascara, and eyebrow plucking to accent her eyes. At first, a girl's efforts to make up her eyes may be clumsy and overdone. Older brothers may tease her about it. Her father may fuss and fume about it. An older sister and her mother can be most helpful by quietly helping her learn how to use eye makeup. School and church youth groups often invite in a cosmetician to help their girls learn how to choose and use makeup for eyes and face in ways that show good taste. The girl who uses no cosmetics can be assured that many attractive women do not have to rely on "bottled beauty." They effect the sweet, clean, natural look so appealing in the younger girl.

Glasses may be important for a girl's ability to see and to read. But she may feel that they detract from her appearance.

When other girls doff their glasses as soon as they are out of the family's sight, it is hard not to follow suit. If a girl believes that "boys seldom make passes at girls who wear glasses," she may prefer blurred vision to being ignored, especially now when she is so eager to be noticed and approved. If a girl's parents are cognizant of how important such things are to a young adolescent girl, they will do all they can to be of assistance. They can back her in selecting attractive frames for her needed lenses. They may even go along with her plea for contact lenses if their doctor recommends them, if they feel they can afford them, and if the girl will be responsible for their care. Such things are matters for family discussion and decision-making. The girl's wishes are important, but they are only one factor. Her sight now and later, what the family can afford, and how both she and her parents feel about it are also important.

Orthodontia is effective in straightening out-of-line teeth. There was a time in earlier generations when a woman went through life with crooked teeth, without a good bite, or with protruding front teeth and other conditions that detracted from her appearance. Now some families find the thousands of dollars needed for tooth-straightening in their pubescent and adolescent children who require it. This is quite a sacrifice for many families. It takes a couple of years more or less. It demands the full cooperation of the youngster to brave the braces and to use the retainers that are necessary.

Good dental health requires regular tooth care. This includes brushing after meals and snacks, the use of dental floss, and checkups by the dentist twice a year. Tooth decay increases during the period of most rapid growth, so keeping teeth clean and sparkling is important both for appearance and for healthy teeth and gums. Children brought up in families where sweets are kept to a minimum and who have snacks of apples, carrot and celery sticks, and other crisp foods rather than soft, sugary, or fat things are fortunate. Regular toothbrushing habits instilled early are an asset to the pubescent girl. A father, who admires his daughter's smile and tells her often how attractive she is, does more than he knows to encourage her in the practices that further enhance her appearance.

It is natural for a girl to want to experiment with a variety of ways of presenting herself. In time she will realize that it is not what she puts on her face, or eyes, or mouth, but what is inside that makes her attractive. Her family's support speeds this process toward inner radiance that is the source of a woman's beauty.

Menstruation—the Monthly Period

Menstruation marks the beginning of womanhood in the eyes of a girl. She has been growing up for some years. Toward the end of the time when she has been growing the fastest, she begins to menstruate. This is a normal function of every woman between puberty and menopause.

The menstrual flow comes from the lining of the uterus, or womb. This is a pear-shaped organ deep in the female pelvis where a baby can grow someday. Each month a thick lining develops inside the uterus to prepare for nourishing a baby. Of course, no baby is growing there most of the time, so this temporary lining of the womb is sloughed off. It appears between the vulva as a bloody discharge.

The amount of blood and mucus discharged each month differs greatly from girl to girl. Some girls menustruate heavily for a week or more. Others have a light flow that lasts only two or three days. Usually a girl menstruates four or five days for a total of little more than a few teaspoonfuls each month.

Periods may not be regular at first. Usually a woman menstruates every twenty-eight days or so, but there are normal differences in the length of the menstrual cycle. Especially when a girl is just beginning to menstruate, irregularity is not unusual. She may menstruate one month, and then skip a month or two or more before her next period comes. Or, she may menstruate more than once in a month. In time, her periods become regular enough so that she knows about when they are to occur. Then she keeps track of them on her personal calendar so that she can plan ahead for her next period.

Preparing for menstruation is important. A family is wise to prepare its daughter for her first menstrual period, before it arrives. As soon as a girl's mother notices that her daughter has entered puberty, she is wise to make sure that the girl is ready for her first period. Sometimes this can easily be discussed by a girl and her mother. At other times a girl is embarrassed, or a mother may not find talking about it an easy thing to do. Mother may give her daughter a book or pamphlet to read and tell her that she will be glad to answer any questions. Mother and father can ask if the school has covered the subject of menstruation in their daughter's health course, or other classes, and then discuss what seems best with the girl.

One mother approached the matter in a woman-to-woman way with her daughter. She invited the girl to go shopping with her one day. Enroute to the shopping center the mother asked her daughter how she would like to select her own menstrual belt and pads that she soon would be needing. The girl wondered how her mother knew she soon would be menstruating. This gave the mother the opportunity to talk about the process of puberal changes, of which menstruation is the most obvious. By the time they reached the store, the two were ready for the girl's choosing of her own sanitary belt and pads. The clerk was helpful, and the experience was a good one for both mother and daughter. From then on, it was easy for the two females of the family to engage in woman talk as they worked together around the house.

Menstrual distress is uncomfortable, for awhile, for some girls. A day or two before the period begins a girl feels "full" or "bloated," as her body retains more water than usual. This may make her cranky and moody unless she knows how to keep herself in good spirits. She may have some cramps the first day of her menstrual period. This does not mean that anything is the matter with her. Usually all that is necessary is to take a mild analgesic like aspirin to dull the pain, and go on as usual. Girls who are anxious about becoming women, or who want to be babied a bit in their fear of growing up often suffer more menstrual discomfort than those who are glad to be developing into womanhood.

Positive ways of keeping menstrual distress to a minimum include getting rid of such "kinky" ideas about menstruation as calling it "the curse," and bemoaning one's fate as a female. Taking the monthly event that all women experience as a normal, natural part of maturity is half the battle against feeling miserable at menstrual time. Keeping oneself exceptionally clean and well-groomed helps give a girl a feeling of being dainty and feminine. The old ideas that it was unsafe to shampoo one's hair or to take a bath when menstruating are nonsense. Now especially a girl wants to be odor-free and nice to be near. She just makes sure that she does not get chilled or overly tired while she is menstruating. Her mother and her doctor can help relieve her anxiety and any distress she is having. The rest is up to her.

Miracle of Maturing

A girl can be pleased and proud that she is growing up. Each new step in her development is a cause for personal celebration. She has looked forward to becoming a young lady for years before she enters puberty. When she was four or five she dressed up in her mother's clothes and pretended she, too, was a grown woman. From time to time ever since, she has thought about how she will be just like, or different from, the mature women she knows—her mother, teachers, neighbors, and leaders. Now she is becoming mature, too, which can be and often is a source of satisfaction to her and to her parents.

Anxieties about a girl's maturing are not unusual. A girl may feel awkward when her body is growing faster than she can manage gracefully. She wonders how long she will be clumsy. When her parents remind her that even the ugly duckling turned into a beautiful swan in time, she wonders how long she will have to be such an ugly duckling herself. She is anxious about whether people will like her, and especially if some fine young man will ever love her enough to want to marry her.

Parents, too, are beset with worries once their daughter reaches puberty. They see how tall and mature she looks, and yet they know that she is not as grown-up as she looks or as she would like to be. They are uneasy about whether they have prepared her for all the hazards she will face as a young lady. They trust her, but have less faith in her ability to cope with dangerous situations to which she is exposed now that she looks so grownup. They want to give her freedom to make her own choices as much as possible, but they dare not let her be as free as she wants to be in many ways.

Sensing the miracle of life gives a girl and her parents a solid base of confidence. Parents who share with their children the wonder of normality provide them with a strong inner security. From the time the newborn arrives in the family, parents can be openly thankful that he or she is normal. With so many things that can go wrong, it is miraculous that a child develops as normally as most do. When maturation is underway, there is a sense of the mystery of life that stirs both parent and young person.

Julie expresses herself well as she voices her appreciation for the guidance she has had in preparing for her own maturation. She says: "It was interesting to learn that I am growing up according to a built-in timetable within myself. I was fascinated to know that all those hormones from the pituitary gland in my head and the ovaries in my abdomen were flowing all through me and turning me from a little girl into a young woman. But, more than the scientific facts, I felt deep inside me the stirring of something new—as I will become as a woman, a wife, and someday a mother myself."

3
Young Man in the Making

Growing up can be, and often is, a strain on a boy, on his family, and on his relationship with his parents. Throughout the second decade of a fellow's life he is neither boy nor man, but a combination of both. He clings to many of his little boy ways at the same time that he vigorously protests about how grown-up he is. One day he is absorbed in a ball game with his buddies, and the next he can't be bothered with such "kid stuff." At one time he is sweet and helpful around home; at another he is harsh with his brothers and sisters, defiant with his parents, and generally disagreeable. Deep inside such a boy may not like himself any more than do his parents just then. But, when he is worried about what is happening, and what is to become of him, his behavior reflects his concern.

Each at His Own Time

Each boy matures at his own rate and begins to grow up in his own time schedule. This is not of his choosing. It is determined by his inherited timetable that starts the process of his maturation when his time has come for growing into manhood. Nothing he or his parents can do can alter this built-in timing. It is initiated by the pituitary gland deep in his head that sends a chemical message called a hormone through his bloodstream. One effect of this new hormone is to rapidly increase the boy's height; another is to activate the sex glands that, over the next few years, will turn the boy into a grown man.

Many a boy is impatient to grow up. He watches his father **31** and older brothers shave and earnestly feels his own face for the first sign of hair. He sees some boys his age shooting up and becoming tall and wishes that he, too, might be tall enough to play basketball and other sports. He worries that he will always be a "shorty" unless some understanding adult reassures him that his time is coming.

Late-developing boys have special problems that can be understood. They appear still to be little boys at the time when other fellows their age are getting taller and looking more like men. They are too short to be of value on the playing field. They are too young-looking to interest the girls their age who usually already are well into pubescence. Late-maturing lads are apt to be unnecessarily anxious about themselves unless their parents interpret to them the usual individual differences between boys their age. Reminding their son that he is much like his father who did not get his full growth until his late teens may be helpful. Even more personally reassuring is guidance into activities where physical stature is not required.

The boy who joins the band or other music group finds an outlet that may be invaluable now and later. Dramatics, science, art, public speaking, mechanics, and a host of other interests may be developed now before a boy's maturation is underway. In fact, he may become a better scholar for being relieved of some of the stresses of social life too soon undertaken by early-developing preteens. Understanding parents can watch for signs of a boy's anxiety about his slow development and guide him into activities that are right for him. A family project of building a boat or a cabin may be just what such a boy needs to bridge over the period until he is well on the way to manhood.

Early maturing boys have somewhat less of a problem than do fellows who begin to mature at a later age. The boy who gets his full height early in his teens feels reassured that he is all right. The other fellows look up to him. The girls his age admire him more than his "little boy" classmates who still seem like such kids. He is invited to join the team in junior high school and to do some of the other things that have status in school and community.

Whenever a boy begins to grow up, he has some problems. His long bones grow so fast that he trips over his own feet and knocks things over with his big hands. He gets moody and snaps back at his parents for no reason they can see except that he feels uneasy within himself. He worries about how his body is functioning, especially in the ways that are hard to talk about with others.

What Happens as a Boy Grows into Manhood

There is a predictable sequence in a boy's maturation that is the same whenever a fellow enters puberty. In general he grows in height before he gets his breadth, and he gains size and weight before he gets his full strength. Each of these aspects of his growth into manhood have implications for him and those who live with him.

Height before breadth is the usual sequence in a boy's early puberty. During the years before he reaches his teens or soon thereafter, depending on the individual, the boy stretches up out of his clothing. His arms hang below the jacket that fit him well just a few months ago. His slacks are suddenly too short. He sits tall in his chair and may tower over his father as he stands beside him. He may increase several inches in a single year—more than he has for the previous several years. This calls for new clothes more often than before. It requires new attitudes on his part and on his family's part. It is obvious now that he is no longer "just a little kid" but a man-in-the-making with all the feelings and responsibilities this implies.

Big hands and feet are part of puberty. Anyone who has ever raised a puppy is familiar with the "all paws" stage of the young dog's growth. The young animal appears out of proportion, with extremities too big for the rest of him for awhile. This same thing happens in young humans, too. Suddenly, the boy's gloves and shoes no longer fit. He seems to be "all thumbs" without the manual dexterity that he once enjoyed. He spills things at the table when he misjudges the distance between his hands and the glass or pitcher. He stumbles and falls, trips and tumbles over "nothing." Fussing at him to be more careful does not help. He must learn anew to use his hands and arms, feet, and legs now so much longer than they used to be. It will take time and patience, both on his part and that of his parents, too. Ridicule only slows his development of adult coordination and damages his self-image as well.

Broader shoulders, tapered chest of manhood follow the stretching up phase of maturation. One sees the adolescent boy throwing back his shoulders with a gesture of pride in their new width. He stretches up out of his narrow waist and expands his chest to its fullest diameter as a way of demonstrating to himself that he is indeed becoming a man in appearance. His upper arms and legs are developing, and he takes pleasure in flexing his muscles and showing anyone he trusts what big biceps he has. This is the stage when he may send away for body-building equipment or sign up for physical education at school or at the YMCA. He enjoys running, swimming, and other sports now, although his endurance in such activities lags behind his interest in them.

Voice changes are an inevitable part of growing up in a boy. As a little boy he had a higher pitched voice than he will have as a man. During puberty, his larynx (voice box or Adam's apple in his throat) becomes larger. This larger size deepens his voice to a lower register than it was before. In time a young man can count on being a tenor, baritone, or bass rather than the boy soprano he once may have been. But until his vocal chords adjust themselves to their new size, the boy may find that his voice is unpredictable. It "cracks" into a new register as he speaks or sings. This often is embarrassing for the fellow.

It is hard enough controlling an unreliable voice without members of one's family making fun of it. Many an adolescent boy wishes that his father and older brothers would not taunt him because of his unsteady voice that squeaks when least expected. The boy who can laugh *with* others who find his unpredictable voice amusing is taking a positive step in adjusting to one of the universal changes all men experience as they grow up.

Size before strength is to be expected in a boy's growth. He increases in height and girth and begins to look like a man before he has a man's strength and endurance. The growth of his heart, lungs, and much of his muscle system takes years to reach their full maturity. Until that time, the adolescent boy tires easily and needs a great deal of rest. His parents may wonder why he slouches in the chair, or why he drapes himself out on the sofa or flops so often on the floor. The reason may simply be that his body "has had it" at the time, and he is giving it the rest it needs.

He needs more sleep now that he is getting his growth. He is growing faster now than he has since he was a preschooler and needs about as much rest as he did then. If he does not get to bed early enough at night, he will awaken with difficulty the next morning. This can cause dissension in the family. If Mother fusses when he does not come on time for the hot breakfast she has prepared for the family, he may not be too pleasant when he finally gropes his way to the table. If Father ridicules him about getting his "beauty sleep" or yells at him for being so lazy, it is not going to help. The only effective way to cope with the growing boy's requirement for rest is to help him get it, with good-humored acceptance of it—by him and his parents.

He is always hungry. This is generally the case with the boy in preteens or teen years who is in his fastest growth spurt. His family may laugh about his having a "hollow leg." IIis mother may seriously wonder if he has a tape worm, he seems so ravenous so much of the time. The family food bills mount, and still he wants more to eat. Now that he is building muscle and bone, he needs more nourishing food than he did before he started to grow up so fast. He needs the calcium of milk and cheese. He needs the vitamins and minerals of fresh fruits and vegetables. He especially needs the meat, fish, eggs, cheese—the high-protein foods—that provide the building-blocks for his growth.

Snacking on "empty calories" does not really satisfy his hunger. It only develops poor eating habits that may make him too fat in time. Potato chips, French fries, and soft drinks are all wrong for the growing lad. They are too full of fats, starches, and sugars, with little that is really good for him. Far better are the apples, carrot sticks, milk, buttermilk, fruit juice, and lean meat that are available for him when he is hungry. Thoughtful parents keep such foods easily available in the refrigerator where he can "piece out" between three well-balanced meals and a bedtime snack. Good food habits are family-made and parent-encouraged through the years.

Hair on face, body, arms, and legs appears as a boy grows up. He is usually proud of the hair that begins to grow in mature patterns on his face and body as he matures. He has anticipated facial hair ever since he first watched his father shave. Now he relishes having to shave, more than he ever will again in all likelihood. He rubs his chin and asks the family quite seriously if they don't think he'd better shave again. They let him down when they observe that there isn't yet fuzz enough to fuss about. What he wants is their assurance that he's a big boy now with the need to keep clean-shaven. A few years later, he will be quite as proud of his first mustache, or long sideburns, or a beard, or whatever is the fashion when he reaches his middle or later teens.

Pubic hair now is growing in a triangle low on the front of his abdomen, and around his genitals. This hair darkens and curls in time in the manner of pubic hair. So, too, is the hair under his arms which becomes darker and curlier as he matures. Most boys and men do nothing about such hair except to keep it clean. The use of deodorants or antiperspirants is usual under the arms after bathing to keep body odors to a minimum. Hair on chest, arms, and legs is seen as further signs of a fellow's masculinity and need not be a cause for worry or comment.

Skin blemishes during puberty are not uncommon. They begin to appear as soon as the body responds to the sex hormones that now are present in the boy's blood stream. One effect of these new chemicals is to stimulate the oil and sweat glands of the skin. The overproduction of oily secretion sometimes clogs the pores of the skin on a boy's face. These may fester into pimples, or become dirt-clogged blackheads. Many a boy spends anguished hours before the bathroom mirror squeezing his blackheads, which is not a good way to treat the problem. This is apt to spread the infection and to bruise the tender tissue around the inflamed pores. Far better is the practice of keeping the face clean with frequent washing with a mild soap and warm water. This should be done morning and evening, and more often if indicated. A diet low in fats and sweets helps keep the skin clear.

Stubborn acne should be called to the attention of a physician who may have the treatment that will be most effective. Going into hiding because one's face is broken out is unfortunate. Better by far is coping with the problem sensibly and living with oneself and others in good grace during puberty and adolescence. When parents and family stand by with encouragement and support, it helps more than they know.

Growth of primary sex organs may be a matter of concern to a boy. He finds other lads his age comparing the size of their male organs and is eager to have his measure up. Boys his age are apt to put a great deal more emphasis on sheer size than is merited. Actually, it makes little or no difference how large a penis is, as long as it functions well. The testes hang suspended in the scrotum behind the penis and grow to their mature size during puberty. They begin to produce the male hormones that bring on other male characteristics. At puberty the testes start the regular production and release of sperm that enable the boy to become a father someday.

Undescended testes may be a worry to a boy. This condition usually rights itself during puberty, if not before. If the testes do not spontaneously drop into the scrotum during the boy's early teens, there is a not-too-complicated medical procedure that can be used. Either one or both of the testes may be involved. It is a matter of little consequence, except as the boy feels about it. The male hormone production goes on in the testis whether it is in the abdomen or in the scrotum.

When a man is ready to become a father, the position of the testes is critical. They must be in the scrotum to protect the sperm from the higher temperatures of the body. Most boys already know that the scrotum contracts close to the body in cold weather, and hangs lower when it is warm. In this way, nature provides the optimum temperature for sperm production.

New Functioning

Becoming mature involves more than just getting bigger— either as a whole person or in any part of one's body. As a boy develops toward manhood, he begins to function as a man. He must learn how to take care of his changing body that is new in size, form, and function now that mature maleness is his.

Smegma is a cheesy secretion that becomes smelly if the penis is not kept clean. Boys who have not been circumcised have to be especially careful to cleanse the end of the penis of any smegma that may have accumulated under the foreskin. From the time a boy was a little lad, his parents have admonished him to wash his private parts carefully as he bathed. This becomes especially important now when he is growing into manhood.

Seminal emissions (wet dreams) are to be expected as a boy develops toward manhood. At night when a boy is sleeping he has a sexy dream that is accompanied by the spontaneous release of semen from his erect penis. This is popularly called a "wet dream." Such nocturnal emissions are natural ways of releasing semen in maturing boys and men. It is not a sign that the boy is losing anything he needs. Nor is it an indication that he has brought it on himself. Seminal emissions are as natural and as spontaneous as a sneeze and need be no more a cause of alarm.

The first time a boy has a seminal emission he may be embarrassed about what to do with his night clothing and bed linen. He can rest assured that his mother and father understand such things and simply go about his business in the usual way.

Masturbation often is a problem for a boy. Parents, too, are apt to be unduly concerned with evidence that their boy is "handling himself." They probably were brought up to think that such behavior is "not nice," "not good for one," or even sinful. They possibly were punished when they were young children for touching their genitals. So when they became adolescents, they felt guilty about masturbating. They may still feel uneasy about it. These feelings get through to their children, even if little or nothing is said about it in the family. So a boy is ashamed of himself when he rubs his penis and wishes he could be strong enough not to have to do it anymore.

Studies show that almost all persons relieve their own sexual tensions when other outlets are not available for them. Maturing boys usually rub the erect penis until it ejaculates. As soon as a boy is mature enough to have semen, it is ejaculated either spontaneously in seminal emissions, in actual sexual encounters with others, or more likely in masturbation. When parents realize that only these three options are open to their son, they are a bit easier about accepting masturbation as a reality.

A boy is fortunate is his parents have prepared him for public opinion about such intimate behavior when he was little. Thus his mother or father, seeing him with his hand on his penis can tell him quietly that he may be excused. They can explain that certain things are private and that sexual activity of any kind is best kept from others' eyes. They can make an effort not to give him the idea that what he is doing is "bad" but simply that it is not done in front of others. This protects him from teachers' punishment in the schoolroom. It prepares him for what he may do when the sexual tensions of puberty and adolescence build up.

Some boys are more concerned about masturbating than others are. There are differences in the amount of sexual stimulation boys feel and in their instinctual energy. There are fellows who throw themselves so completely into other interests and projects that they have little time for worrying about their bodies. Then, too, some boys are more adequately prepared for their own maturing than are others who feel uncertain about what is happening to them. Getting one's facts straight is one step toward healthy coping with one's own inner urges. The next is becoming involved in life around oneself in ways that assure continued growth and development as a whole person. Parents can be helpful in giving their son a wholesome outlook and in encouraging him in the pursuit of a wide variety of interests and activities.

Myths about masturbation need not to be taken as gospel truth. Contrary to what a boy and his parents may have heard, there is no harm in handling one's genitals except the guilty feelings that one may have about doing it.

Masturbation is a normal and natural part of growing up. It has the advantage of releasing tension as it builds up without hurting anyone else. It helps an individual learn about his own functioning and have respect for his God-given body.

Who Can a Boy Talk To?

Everyone needs someone with whom to share one's personal concerns, hopes, and feelings. During puberty and adolescence a boy needs more than ever a sense of being understood for what he is and is becoming. This comes best from his family and from one or more special pals about his own age.

Parents as confidants are fortunate. They have earned their son's trust, and have built a solid system of communication with him over the years he has been growing up. They make themselves available to him and are able to listen to what he is trying to tell them. A boy who can go to his parents with tales of what is happening to him at school, in the neighborhood, and in his own private life has advantages many other fellows lack. He can talk out his worries before they become too much for him. He can get straight the many things he needs to understand fully now that he is becoming a man. He can accept himself as a worthy human being, too uniquely precious to throw away in irresponsible behavior.

A boy's special pal has a special place in his life when he is entering maturity. The two buddies can share with one another the many new events and experiences they are going through at about the same time. They can, and do, talk about their teachers and the subjects they are taking at school. They share feelings they have about their brothers and sisters, mothers and fathers, grandparents, and others in their families. They develop their own special language with one another and enter into secret pacts that share some of the mystery of communication with another human being. A special pal is an asset in a boy's development that his parents do well to encourage. The other lad may not be perfect in every way, but if their son takes to him, he must be somebody he needs right now.

Close friends during puberty are usually those of about the same stage of development. The early-developing boy may have more in common with a somewhat older boy who is about his own level of development. The late-maturing lad may feel more comfortable with a pal a bit younger who is developmentally on a par with him. Usually the two have several interests in common. They both like to build things. They get interested in one another through a science project. Musical interests draw other pals together. Sports and neighborhood games attract boys with similar interests. As the boys come together in pursuit of their mutual interests, they become involved with one another in a close-knit friendship. Chances are that the two come from somewhat similar families and live not too far from one another. They are lucky lads if their parents accept them as pals and welcome in both their homes.

Fears of homosexuality are generally unfounded at this age. Parents may hesitate to encourage or even allow their son's association with his best friend, especially when their relationship seems so all-absorbing. They are afraid that their boy may be entering into a homosexual attachment that will damage him for life. So much is made of homosexuality that many adults look askance at any close attachment between members of the same sex. Such parents need to be reassured that homosexuality does not stem from the close contacts of pubescent or adolescent boys. If it is present at all, usually it dates back to the boy's early development in the family.

As boys begin to leave childhood behind them, they are naturally drawn to one another. This is a perfectly normal, universal phase of development. They are closer now to members of their own sex of about their age than they were before or probably ever will be again. They are too young and uncertain to dare to have much interest in girls, especially since girls their age are so much more mature and sophisticated than they are. They are not yet ready for more grown-up social life, and they know it. So they tease girls or leave them alone. They form tight little groups of boys their own age in clubs or secret organizations in which they can be free to be themselves.

Clubhouse, boy's room, or basement den come into its own at this age. Here in their hideaway, the boys can be on their own for awhile. Here they discuss their innermost thoughts and feelings. Here they make plans together for bigger and better projects ahead. Here in such a setting a boy can begin to find himself anew as a young-man-in-the-making. With so much happening so fast inside the young adolescent, he needs a safe place in which he can feel secure with those his own age who understand him.

Father-son programs at church, the local YMCA, boys' club, or community center are helpful at this age. Fathers and their boys go on outings together, build canoes, repair automobiles, work for community improvement, and in the process get close to one another. Boys need fathers as male models in living. They like to feel understood by their dads, and to know that their parents respect them as persons. They want to have adults listen to them, even when they are not quite sure what it is that they are trying to say.

Fathers and sons together attend sessions on growing into manhood in many communities. This gives them both the knowledge they need about what is happening to pubescent boys. It provides father and son with the words they need for the questions they both would like to ask.

It gives them both the assurance that it is all right to talk about such things. There is a natural reticence in discussing the mysteries of life that makes it hard for a father to talk candidly with his son. A boy often does not know how to ask the questions that bother him most. Neither of them may have the courage they need to broach such subjects until some common experience makes it seem appropriate. Once the door has been opened for them, they find new satisfaction in one another and in their more open relationship.

Parents encourage family discussion of growing up in a variety of ways. They have brought up their children to come to them with any questions they may have. They take time to listen to the music as well as the words of their sons' and daughters' concerns. They have learned to ask, How did you feel about that? as a way of helping their children identify their own feelings about all sorts of things. They keep abreast of what is happening to their children and so are not shocked with whatever comes up for discussion.

Parents often find books and pamphlets on growing up helpful to both their adolescents and themselves. Such materials are readily available in both church and public libraries. They are found on the tables of denominational publishing houses. It is not hard to find what a mother or father is looking for in most instances. All one has to say is, "My son is growing up—what will be most helpful for him, and me, now?" The alert librarian or clerk can put out a number of possible books from which can be chosen the one or two that seem best at the time.

It is wise for parents to read materials they have brought home for their growing young people. Then they can lay them on the table with a simple announcement that they found them interesting and others in the family may, too. Or, a father may present such a book to his son as something he found for him. The boy's parents probably will want to invite questions about anything in the written material that their son wants to bring up for further discussion. They should not be surprised if the boy protests, "Aw, Mom, I know all that stuff already." The calm response, "It never hurts to review what is known from time to time," makes the parent's position clear at the same time that it saves face for the boy. Few fellows want to admit that there is anything they do not know about boys and sex and growing up. Yet, studies show that almost all boys need, and want, a great deal more knowledge and much more understanding about growing up than is available to them.

There is a wonder about becoming a man that is like no other. Once a boy, now a young man-in-the-making is a fascinating stage of development. It is full of challenge, full of problems, full of hopes, fears, and dreams. It is a period full of potentialities for the boy, his parents, and their relationship.

4
Teens Are Trying Times

The teen years are trying for most young people. In many ways the second decade of life is especially difficult. So many things are happening all at once. So much must be accomplished in order to attain full adulthood. Childish ways must be outgrown, and more mature patterns of behaving have to be learned so well that they become part of a person. Other people expect more of a person once he or she begins to look big and grown-up. Sometimes these expectations are too great, and a teenager gets discouraged with his inability to measure up. Sometimes adults expect too little of teenagers, tending to belittle them and to keep them dependent.

Conflicting demands and pressures impinge upon teenagers from every side. Classmates and neighborhood youth press their peers to conform to the group mores of the moment. These ways often conflict with what other young people and adults in church and family insist upon. Many a teenager is torn between risking being labelled "a square" in refusing to go along with what "all the other kids are doing" and defying his parents and other caring persons who want him to do what is right.

Teenagers' feelings and loyalties shift with confusing frequency. It is a wise teenager who can truthfully answer the question, How do you feel? It is even harder to reply to the query, Why do you feel the way you do? With increasing maturity, a teenager comes to understand himself and his emotions to the place where he knows who his real friends are and what he can count on in them and in himself. But **45** this takes some doing. It is only part of all that teenagers must do in order to find themselves.

What Teenagers Are Trying to Do

Studies of human development through the second decade of life have been reported over the past fifty years or more. They tell a great deal about what younger and older adolescent boys and girls are going through. They suggest some of the reasons teenagers act the way they do, how much of their behavior as adolescents can be expected to carry over into manhood and womanhood, and what probably will be outgrown as adults.

Teenagers find reassuring the knowledge of what is going on as young people. They often get discouraged with themselves and are sometimes baffled by their own behavior. Knowing in general what they are trying to accomplish helps a young person unravel the tangle he is in within a specific situation.

"Why am I so mean to my own mother?" asks fifteen-year-old Marlena. She goes on to say with tear-moistened eyes that her mother is the best friend she ever had, who will do anything for her that is reasonable. Yet Marlena finds herself talking back to her mother, criticizing her in front of the younger children in the family, and refusing to do even the simplest things her mother asks her to do. Marlena is upset by the way she has been behaving and cannot understand why she acts as she does. Fortunately, her counselor is able to explain how all teenagers have to push off their parents' ministrations in order to grow up as independent persons. When mother and daughter have had a particularly good relationship, this declaration of independence may be painful, not only for Mother, but for daughter as well.

Parents understand their teenagers' seemingly irrational behavior when they know what to expect of adolescents and of themselves. Knowledge of the growth responsibilities of young people through the second decade of life is helpful to the adults who live and work with them. With it an adult can realize why the most delightful children often become such disagreeable teenagers. This provides the perspective many a parent desperately needs in order to weather the storms of adolescence in the family.

Pushing off parents is a normal part of growing up. It has been going on for some years but reaches climactic proportions during the teen years. Most children begin to assert themselves early in childhood. Two-and-one-half-year-old Edna pushed her mother away as her coat was being buttoned with a no uncertain, "I can bucken my own coat." Now thirteen, Edna is still pushing off her mother's help in clothing and many other things as well. Before she is twenty, Edna will undoubtedly resist her parents' direction of her life in most areas as she makes more and more of the decisions that concern her.

A young person has to declare his or her own independence as fully as possible during the teen years. By the time young adulthood comes an individual should be using his or her own judgment and living his own life on his own terms. Otherwise, he or she is in danger of being tied too closely to his parents and relying too heavily on their guidance.

Emancipating oneself from one's parents is not easy for a teenager. It is hard to let go the loving care parents have given their children through the years. It is frightening to realize that life's most difficult hurdles lie ahead at the very time that a teenager feels he has to make it on his own. It is scary to dive into some of the world's most complicated situations and leave behind the security of one's home. Just when the most important steps of a teenager's life have to be made, his parents who know him best cannot be allowed to take charge. To finish or to drop out of school, to go on to college or some other training for the future, to go into military or civic service, to follow family patterns of personal behavior, or to rebel into something completely different are some of the major choices facing youth.

Parents long to be consulted and to be assured that their children, in whom they have invested so much, are making the right choices. But they cannot follow their teenagers into the future. They must let them go and grow as persons in their own right. This means letting them make their own decisions, knowing that they will make mistakes. Wise parents have been giving their children the freedom to choose many things for themselves all through the years. This has given their sons and daughters experience in decision-making. It probably has provided the parents with the confidence in their children that both generations need.

Becoming acceptable to peers is a universal effort on the part of teenagers. They yearn to be considered attractive by boys and girls their own age. They would like to be invited into social groups of compatible young people. They need close personal friends of both sexes with whom they can establish mutually pleasant relationships. As they push off from their parents, they gravitate toward friends of their own age with whom they can share confidences and from whom they can get emotional support.

Groups of young people tend to have rigid standards of what is acceptable teenage behavior. They "put down" the too aggressive girl who pushes in where she is not wanted. They tend to ignore the retiring boy or girl who is too shy. They often are cruel in ridiculing the nonconformist and demand conformity beyond anything parents consider appropriate. That is one reason why clothes, hair styles, and grooming tend to be of such exaggerated importance during the teen years. Parents who understand the desire of their adolescents to look like the other young people in the community learn to go along with the styles of the moment insofar as they can.

Learning from social rebuffs and rebukes. Studies over many years find that adolescents generally worry about being left out. They are sad when they are not invited to join a club or to attend a social event. A girl is humiliated by her boyfriend's two-timing. A fellow is apt to "lose his cool" when his girl friend stands him up. Members of both sexes are afraid of making social *faux pas.* They go to great lengths to avoid being ridiculed. Yet these things happen to most young people at one time or another. It takes years to develop the social poise most young adults need to feel at home in the many situations in which they find themselves. In the meantime, there is bound to be embarrassment at times. It takes a great deal of courage to go out to others in friendly, effective ways. It helps to have parents who understandingly stand by with the help and encouragement teenagers need in their expanding social life.

Adjusting to changing physical features, as puberty becomes adolescence, causes boys and girls to go through moments of personal uncertainty. They lengthen out and shoot up in height faster than they have since they were very young children. Their arms and legs stretch out of sleeves and slacks, and the added inches make it hard to gauge distances in reaching, grasping, and holding objects. Things drop and are spilled with disconcerting frequency. The once well-coordinated child often becomes a bumbling adolescent with a body he or she is not yet sure of.

Teenagers worry about certain of their features being out of proportion with others. A boy feels his nose has become too big. A girl tucks her chin into her turtleneck sweater because it seems to her to be disproportionately long. As adult characteristics replace the familiar lines of childhood, each teenager has to become acquainted with himself or herself anew. Louella softens her hair style to mask the new squareness her face has developed. Herb spends time in front of the mirror combing his hair over his ears that appear to have grown too big and stick out too far. One youth feels he is too short, another too tall. Whatever the particular self-criticism, it is usually exaggerated beyond its significance, especially now when appearance is so important and changes so fast.

Adolescence brings not only changes in size but also in shape, function, feeling, and others' expectations. A girl may long for a rounded bust, only to feel "bumpy in front" as her breasts develop. A boy may look forward to becoming bigger, only to be aware of how long his neck has become. It takes time to adjust to such rapid change in size and shape as comes with adolescence, especially when one's body is behaving in new ways.

Learning to function as an adult female or male is even more complicated. As girls begin to menstruate, they are concerned about how frequent, how copious, and how regular their periods should be. They are often preoccupied with caring for themselves in the new ways required of them as maturing young women. They are helped by mothers and older sisters, teachers, and school nurses who know what it is like to be confronted with what it means to be physically mature for the first time.

Boys' worries are apt to be even more severe at this time of life. Research indicates that boys are less well prepared for growing up than are girls. Yet they are expected to know a great deal about life and sex and manhood that no one has told them. Many a fellow is unprepared for his first nocturnal emission and so fears that he may have hurt himself or lost something vital to his manhood. Guilt and shame about masturbation, instilled with the best of intentions, are a heavy burden on a lad. If his father can assure him that there is nothing to worry about, if his doctor can tell him what is normal and natural in male behavior, he can be spared sleepless hours and unnecessary worry.

Recognizing instinctual awakening for what it is spares youth of both sexes some of the anguish of growing up. Both boy and girl from time to time experience new feelings associated with their maturing. A boy has an unexpected erection while looking at a magazine, or touching a girl (accidentally or intentionally). A member of either sex is overcome with desire that quickens breathing, brings a flush to the skin, and wets the armpits—at an unexpected time, place, and stimulus. Unless the young person has been somewhat prepared for these new sensations associated with maturity, he or she may mistake sexual awakening for love and desire for something deeper. Recognizing such feelings in others as well as in oneself is especially helpful now.

Youth today recognize these things more easily than did their parents and grandparents in their time. Today's teenagers talk freely about "having the hots," "getting a crush on," or "falling for" another person to whom they are sexually attracted without having to make a grand romance out of it. When their friends and family openly discuss these things, teenagers come in time to manage their impulses with increasing maturity.

Becoming an independent person is an essential developmental task of teenagers. They enter adolescence as dependent children. Throughout the teen years, they must declare their independence in order to emerge as young adults capable of standing on their own feet and living their own lives. As adulthood arrives, the thrust toward independence subsides and awareness of the interdependence of oneself on others emerges. This requires a sturdy sense of self. The development of which is a central responsibility of each individual during the teen years.

Each young person searches for a sense of his own identity. He or she asks, Who am I? as he compares himself to others and attempts to establish his own uniqueness as an individual. He or she attempts to find his strengths and weaknesses, what he can or cannot do, in what he is or is not talented or interested. He tries out a variety of activities in order to discover in what he excels, what brings him satisfaction, what seems to be his "thing." This is one of the bases for the lack of persistence that parents bemoan in their teenagers. Enthusiasms arise for some new project, only to wane soon after. The family spends more than it should for a musical instrument, only to have it lie unused after an all too brief period. Such conduct strains the family budget and parents' patience. But underneath is the teenager's search for his strengths and what feels right to him.

A youth must bounce his emerging sense of who he is off other persons' ideas, experiences, and values. In this encounter, parents rank high since they are closest to their teenagers and have been their greatest influence through the years of their lives up to now. As youngsters strain away from being little mirror images of their parents, they must in some measure repudiate some of the aspects of their parents' lives. They rebel from whatever in their parents' generation they find inacceptable: materialism, hypocrisy, war, famine, paternalism, or whatever.

The teenage daughter becomes openly critical of her mother's appearance, the way she does her hair, or manages her wardrobe. This is hard for many a mother to take, especially when she tends to neglect herself in order to give her daughter what she needs and wants. Studies find that by the middle teens, girls tend to be most highly critical of their mothers, as persons, as wives, and as mothers. This is hard on Mother and on her relationship with her daughter. It can be softened by the realization that what the girl is trying to do is to differentiate herself from the model of womanhood with which she has grown up, and to which she is so attached—her own mother.

Listen and Understand

Teenagers tend to feel that no one understands them, partly because they do not fully understand themselves, partly because others do not appear to listen as closely as they might. *Being understood is crucial* to one's feeling of being cared for by those to whom one turns. Emily in Thornton Wilder's play, *Our Town*, beseeches her mother, "Listen to me; look at me, Mother," as her mother busies herself with her housework while Emily wants desperately to be seen and heard and understood. It is easy to be preoccupied when those nearby have need of one's full attention. Adolescents close themselves in their rooms and turn their record players up to drown out the voices of the family. Mothers lose themselves in their work at home, church, or community. Fathers absent themselves even when they are at home by getting lost behind the daily paper. Sometimes all this is a deliberate effort to avoid an unpleasant scene. More often it is a lack of competence in handling delicate human relations.

Listening is hard work. As any social worker or minister can tell you, really listening to what another person is saying is difficult. Your mind wanders to what you have to do later. Your concentration is broken by thoughts of what you will say as soon as the other person has finished talking. You hear the words the other individual is speaking, but you miss the main message. Truly listening to another human being involves hearing not only what he says, but sensing what it means to him. You have to become aware of the feelings back of what is being said in order to listen in the fullest sense. This is why counselors so often respond, "How did you feel about that?" This helps the trained listener understand what the situation meant to the person involved. Even more, it enables the troubled person to sort out his feelings and to clarify for himself what is going on in his life right now.

Family listening is essential for a sense of well-being. When a teenager feels that his parents have heard him out and sense what he is going through, he feels better, even if they cannot do anything about his current dilemma. Close families are usually those in which the art of listening has become well-established within the home. Parents and children take time for one another. They keep tuned in on what is happening to the others in the family so that they are in on any new developments and changes that take place.

Understanding is a two-way process. It includes attempting to understand the other person as best you can. And, it involves making yourself clear and understandable. Impatience is an enemy of understanding. It cuts off communication at the very time when it is most needed. The teenager who slams the door with an impatient "You just don't understand" is cutting himself off from the communication he wants. Such an accusation repulses his parents and widens the gulf between the generations.

One father expressed himself explosively on the matter when he said: "Hear this. I got through the depression. I survived two wars and the periods of cold war in between. I've learned to live with an ulcer, crumbling teeth, thinning hair, bad investments, complaining kids, and mounting family costs. I've had to cope with inflation, the threat of bankruptcy, and high taxes. I'm disillusioned about governmental dishonesty, cover-ups, and chicanery. So, no smart-aleck teenager is going to tell me that I don't know what life is all about." This may sound like an harangue but it served to sober his teenaged son, to the point of an almost-apology: "Gosh, Dad, I didn't mean to set you off. I only wanted to get you to hear what I'm going through right now."

Making oneself understood is one facet of being understood. You cannot expect that others will know what you are thinking or how you are feeling if you do not attempt to tell them. The father's verbal explosion above had the effect of showing his son what the father's life had been like. His son's response served to open the door to further communication between them. As soon as the boy openly admitted that he was going through something difficult to handle, he had his father's attention. The man, in turn, felt better for having expressed himself so fully and could listen to his son's problems.

"This means a lot to me" is one way of getting others' attentive listening. Teenage Janice found that she could approach either of her parents with an appeal for their help with anything she found troublesome. All she had to do was to say: "When you have time, I have something important to talk over with you. This means a lot to me, so I want you to really listen to me." This got her parents' full attention and enabled the family to discuss the problem on which she needed their help. This was far more effective than a childish complaint that they did not listen to her. For it was positive,

direct, and immediate in establishing communication within the family.

Being Responsive to Uniqueness

In the heat of an argument, teenagers have been known to accuse their elders of being all alike. Annoyed adults sometimes lump all young people into the "crazy kids" category. Such labelling of members of a whole generation is rarely helpful. In using such broad generalizations of an entire age group, the individual is diminished, and the facts of the case are distorted.

Each responds in his own way. Most young people actually know that adults are not alike. Some older and younger individuals are sensitive and responsive. Some are easy and others hard to talk to. Some are firm, others are lenient. Members of both generations are alike only in their being human beings doing what they can to meet their own basic needs. It is safe to assume that persons are at work on their own personal developmental tasks that vary throughout the life-cycle, and for each individual of whatever age.

Each individual was born uniquely himself or herself, like no other person who is or ever was. From birth onward, each person becomes more and more himself or herself. No two individuals have the same experiences, even in the same family. Each one responds in his or her own way to what happens, thereby further expressing his uniqueness, and making his individuality even more solidly a part of him.

Individual differences make each person special. In a very real way each individual is irreplaceable. No one else can be or do or think or feel in exactly the same way. Democracy in the nation or in the family encourages the development and expression of individual differences. This is a source of strength for the person and for the group. It also is one basis for some of the tension that arises from time to time between members of the family, the community, the country, or the world.

Why don't you do as I would? is an empty question, that is very easily answered. I do not do as you would in a like situation, because I am not you. I am *me*, and must act as I do because I am what I am. One mother we knew had a favorite expression whenever one of her children did something she did not like. It was, "I would not do a thing like that." When one of her sons was but a little lad, he responded with wisdom beyond his years with: "Of course not, Mom. Mothers act like mothers, but a boy has to be a boy."

Being responsive to the uniqueness of each individual in each situation is one secret of happy family living. In a good home, each member of the family feels safe to be himself. Each feels free to express his own true feelings, whatever they may be. Each assumes that others may not see things as he does because they too are uniquely themselves. So each makes a conscious effort to get the wavelength of the others in order that he may receive what is being sent as that person's signal. Think of it as a code that each person communicates with, a code that must be broken if he or she is to be understood.

Trying Times in the Family

The teen years are trying times because so much is being accomplished in the period between childhood and maturity. This is the decade in which each young person must grow up in his or her own way, doing his or her own thing, and at his or her own pace. This requires effort and real working on with an intensity beyond any family chore or lessons at school. It continues through the years as the central set of tasks each teenager sets for himself. It is the complex of things he *must* do if he is to continue to grow toward his own next step in development.

Teenagers are trying, in a double sense. They are trying to mature, and they are trying to live with at times. Parents can openly admit that they sometimes find their youngsters exasperating. But they can make the teen years easier for themselves and for their adolescent sons and daughters by reminding themselves that teenagers are young but a few years more. In time, even the most moody adolescent grows out of the emotional turmoil of trying to grow up. In time, too, parents become less trying to their teenagers.

Parents can relax more than they realize as their children go through the teen years. The family has left its imprint on its sons and daughters. The parents have done what they could throughout the early formative years of each child's life. Now it is time for them to hold their children with an open hand, letting them be free to go and grow and find themselves. This means standing by as a base of security when it is needed. It means being available for guidance when it is requested. It means becoming more mature persons as man and woman, husband and wife, as well as father and mother. It means being the kind of adults that set a worthy example for the younger members of the family. More than they know, it is what they are rather than what they say that impresses teenagers. Parents and teenagers find the teen years less trying when parents do not try too hard. These are the years to trust teenagers to work things through with less and less parental assistance. This is the time when parents and teenagers can enjoy the fruits of freedom, with mutual respect and faith in one another.

5
Parents Are Trying Too

While their teenagers are trying to become mature young men and women, parents are hard at work on their own tasks as adults. They face new challenges as parents of older children, as marriage partners, and as middle-aged men and women. Attention is so focused on what youth is trying to do, that what is happening to Mother and Father is often overlooked by their children and by themselves. Yet they are the key figures in their teenagers' development toward maturity. What they are going through directly affects their sons and daughters.

Tasks of Teenagers' Parents

The day begins in many a family with the query, What are you going to do today? Mother's response is often in terms of places she must go and things she must do around the house. Father's reply is usually in terms of his work and his chores around the home. Beneath these mundane jobs lie the basic tasks of the couple whose child-rearing has reached a new stage of life, as indeed they have themselves. Now they must tackle a number of developmental responsibilities that must be accomplished if they are to go successfully on to their next stage of the family life-cycle.

Paying the bills when costs zoom is a crucial task of teenagers' parents. These are the days when family food costs are higher than they ever have been. Teenage boys are always hungry, and their adolescent sisters have higher nutritional needs than they have had since they were little youngsters.

Food fads, special diets, and having friends in from time to time put further strains on the family food budget. Clothing of even the simplest sort is expensive today, and the variety of appropriate wear for social events, school, sports, and work is usually greater for teenagers than for young children or adults. Transportation takes a big bite from the family exchequer in the years while there are teenagers at home. Automobiles get more mileage, auto insurance rates are higher when the car is driven by those under twenty-one, and cash outlay for regular and special trips by automobile, bus, plane, or train is costly. Add to this the expense of tooth-straightening, eye examinations and glasses, accidents, illness, and all the other expected and unexpected expenses, and you see the financial pinch of a family with teenagers.

Future costs loom even larger among families who expect their sons and daughters to go on for further education beyond high school. College costs are higher now than they have ever been, and many young people aspire not only to four years of college but to graduate and professional study as well. So parents tighten their belts and find other sources of income beyond those tapped to date.

Maintaining a comfortable home amid the normal wear and tear of an active family is an expected task of teenagers' parents. Older children become critical of familiar furnishings and press for nicer carpeting, furniture, and equipment. Teenagers and their friends give the home hard wear as they traipse through for snacks, meals, parties, and after-game functions. Most parents would rather their young people would come home for their fun than go out to commercial establishments. They recognize that things must be nice enough to make it easy for their children to invite friends in without embarrassment. The problem becomes acute when teenagers do not take care of what is already there. Clothes left in a heap, stains on carpeting, rings left on polished furniture, and a general air of messiness increase work for Mother and the possibility of intensified tension in the home.

Looking after older relatives is assumed as a responsibility by most men and women whose children are teenagers. By now their own parents are older with some of the special needs of the aging for the loving attention of their adult children. In some families a widowed grandmother is made to feel at home with the family, putting the parents in the middle between the younger and older generations. More often the grandparents live separately with regular contact with their married children and grandchildren. Gifts are exchanged, vacations are taken together, holidays are celebrated as a whole family, with all the joys and complexities of three- and four-generation relationships. Now that more adults live out their full life span, there are great-grandparents, elderly aunts and uncles, cousins, and other older kinfolk to further extend the family.

Participating in church and community is an ongoing effort of teenagers' parents. Their teenage children may go willingly to church, or they may resist going for awhile. Weekend trips and family outings tempt the family away from regular Sunday services, but the parents usually try to maintain their membership. They often are drawn into community drives of one kind and another. They serve on boards, get elected to positions of responsibility, and carry out their role as responsible citizens as fully as they can. All this takes some doing with all the other demands on their time and energy.

Guiding younger and older children continues while there are teenagers in the family. The teenage son or daughter may help with the care and guidance of younger brothers and sisters. Or, as happens more often than is recognized, they would rather not be bothered with tag-along younger members of the family.

Studies find that by the middle teens a girl is more critical of the way her parents are raising the younger children in the home than she has ever been before. She may challenge their authority in front of her younger siblings, thus increasing the problems their parents have in childrearing. Older brothers and sisters serve as models for good or ill on the teenagers still at home.

Not long after Tom had been apprehended for the possession of drugs, his teenage sister was found smoking pot. Her parents were upset, of course, not only by what she was doing, but especially by her attitude. She boldly told them, "If Tom does it, it must be all right." Her parents had always been proud of Tom, and happy that the younger children in the family looked up to him. But now this—what could they do about it? It was not until Tom himself hit bottom, and realized the extent of what he had done that the family got back on an even keel again.

Some parents have the problem of so admiring an older son or daughter that they expect too much of their younger children as they come along. Susan had been a straight A student all through school. She had been active in church and a leader of youth groups in town. When her younger sister, Beth, became a teenager, she was up against the admirable reputation Susan had made at school and in the family. Beth's teachers reminded her all too often that her grades did not match those of Susan. Her parents had a hard time not comparing the two girls as they tried to accept and encourage their less-talented younger daughter. When the older sibling has been a popular sports figure, well-known in music, drama, or other activities, the parents' problem of balancing their pride of the older without unfavorable comparison of the younger is very real.

Finding themselves as a couple heading into the middle years of their marriage is a task of great importance to them and to the family as a whole. The middle-aged woman is apt to compare herself unfavorably with her attractive teenage daughter. She may feel dowdy, not-too-smart, and out-of-date in the face of the expressed superiority of her teenage children and their friends. The man in his forties, old enough to have teenage children, is said to be in his "dangerous years." He sees his youth slipping away from him, and he may be tempted to make one last effort to enjoy himself while there is yet time. His life appears humdrum, his work too demanding, and his pleasures all too few, unless he has been fortunate in fulfilling his own needs as a grown man as well as a father.

By the time a couple have teenage children they have been married for years. The first blush of excitement has gone, and the old romance may be hard to capture now that they have become so accustomed to one another. The wife may not appear quite so cute and stylish as some of "the girls" at work. The wife's fantasies may be filled with men more exciting than those of her "dear old Joe." Husband or wife may chafe under the harness of daily demands each wears. He may yearn for a job more to his liking. She may want to take a course or two and develop talents too long pushed aside. They come together with their individual aspirations and frustrations as well as their need for one another's support. It is a loving husband who can encourage his wife to do the things that mean much to her without too great an emphasis on what he is sacrificing in involvement in activities beyond him and the home. It is a faithful wife who can hear out her husband's concerns enough to sense when he is only griping temporarily and when he needs her backing to plunge into the new location or career that will give him the fresh lease on life he needs.

Research indicates that during the period when there are teenagers in the family, communication between husband and wife tends to improve. The parents are drawn together by their mutual need for one another, and by their common concern for their teenagers. They confide in one another during the night hours while they await homecoming teenagers. They find a new depth of their relationship growing out of their efforts to find themselves, and one another again—if they are lucky.

Teens Are Tough on Parents

Many parents dread the teen years even before their children reach them. They remember their own stormy adolescence and would like to spare their children the anguish they went through. They are not proud of the way they treated their parents when they were in their teens and yet cannot hope that their youngsters will spare them similar indignities in their time. They feel uncertain about their adolescents, and they are not sure of themselves. Even when they are sure of their ground, they hesitate to put down a parental foot too hard for fear of alienating their youngsters just when they are most needed.

To split means to get out. One father tells how his memories of his own teen years got in the way of his controlling his teenage son. The boy had been rude, disrespectful, and in need of a good old-fashioned scolding, as the father recounts it. So Dad worked himself up to a fine pitch and was really letting the boy "have it." At which the youngster sullenly said that there was no pleasing the old man any more, that nothing he did was right in his dad's eyes. His eyes flashed with indignation, and he flung out the door, saying, "I might as well split." The father's first reaction was, "Good riddance." Then he began to have second thoughts: Where is he going?, What will he do?, What have I driven him into, with my angry tirade? He had a flashback to a similar episode with his own father when he had slammed the door with a final shout: "All right, if I am such a mess, I might as well get out." He had walked for miles, slept in a friend's house, and crept back home late the next day with a hangover, and a bad case of guilt-ridden jitters. It was not a happy reminder of what his own son might be going through right now.

Times have changed since parents were young. They know it, and their teenagers often remind them of it. Whereas Father in his day ran to a friend and the defiant solace of drinking, today's teenagers have a wider variety of far more dangerous escapes. They can travel miles beyond their home territory and consort with people like those their parents never knew. They can fall prey to a myriad of exploitive associates and strangers in almost any direction in which they turn. Hardly a day goes by without its gruesome headline of some youngster picked up on the highway, mugged on the street, bloody in some isolated woods, bedded down with someone of either sex, or hooked by some dope peddler. It's enough to make a conscientious parent's blood run cold to acknowledge such contemporary possibilities that lie beyond the family's front door.

Discipline is difficult when parents are afraid of driving their teenagers away from home before they are ready to cope with life on their own. Young persons seem ready to cast off their parents' concern like an outgrown garment. Understandably, a parent may be uncertain as to how much pressure to exert on his son and daughter without losing them entirely.

Rosalee has been "asking for it" for some time now. She has been quarrelsome with her sister and openly hostile to her mother. Her foul language is unlike anything allowed in the family. She avoids her father whenever she can and "puts down" her mother with remarks that border on the insulting. Thus far, Rosalee's mother has tried to ignore her own hurt in an effort to keep the situation from becoming explosive. She does not want to drive her daughter from her home when she is most vulnerable. So she pretends not to hear her daughter's outbursts in the hope that they will lessen in time. But they only get more abusive, until the family is in a continual state of tension.

Understanding what is going on through the teen years often is a first step toward knowing what to do about them—both as teenagers and as parents. That is the reason members of both generations can be helped by study of adolescent development and the changing relationships between the generations through the teen years.

Fifteen and Fifty—Explosive!

"Just when I need a little peace and quiet in my life, I have to have a noisy adolescent!" This explosion was surprising coming from cool, calm, unflappable Claire. She was a loving mother and usually a most understanding person. But her boisterous teenagers were more than she could stand. Her head ached, her hands developed a slight tremor, and she wondered if she were cracking up. Her doctor to whom she had turned in desperation, reminded her that her menopause had altered the hormonal balance of her body and that she was reacting as a woman in the change of life sometimes does. He prescribed a daily dosage of estrogen to replace those her body was not supplying in adequate quantities. He reassured her that her feelings were within the range of the normal and that she would feel better when she took some time off for herself—in restful pursuits that she found relaxing and fulfilling.

Adolescence and menopause are both unstable times. It is during the teen years that chemical changes in the young person's body alter the way he or she feels. This is an uneasy time emotionally when feelings outdistance controls, when tempers flare and voices are raised. This period in the lives of adolescents all too often coincides with Mother's menopause. This is the change in the woman's life when her active repro-ductive life draws to a close, her menstruals taper off, and her hormonal balance is temporarily out of kilter. The meno-pausal woman tends to be unstable partly because her chemis-try is changing and partly because she is going from one phase of her life to the next. At a time when Mother is trying to get herself under control, she finds herself living with one or more teenagers who are as easily upset as she is. This makes for an ever-changing emotional climate in which tears are shed and confrontations are inevitable. In time, Mother calms down, and teenagers emerge as thoughtful, considerate young adults. But throughout the teen years there may be storms and high pressure areas that disturb the climate of even the finest family.

Mother is an example for the others in the family in the way she manages her "bad days." She takes out her discomfort on the other family members in unpleasant ways, and they learn to avoid her to escape her criticism. Or, she tips off the family that she is under the weather, so that they and she can cope realistically with her periodic upsets. She comes to breakfast with a smile and a warning: "Be careful, I am not at my best this morning." This reassures her husband and children that her mood is not of their making. It gives them a chance to express the loving concern that will make her and the rest of the family feel better.

Teenagers have off days too. As Carl puts it: "Some days nothing seems to go right. You wake up feeling uncomfortable about what happened last night. Your best slacks are too dirty to wear. Your bike pedal comes off as you start for school. You miss a question you thought you knew. Your best friend is too busy to listen. Your girl friend cuts you cold. Everything you touch seems to go bad on you. On top of all that, your folks bug you about a lot of little things. No one seems to care what happens to you. You get the blues and only make things worse for yourself, and everybody else." This not unfamiliar pile-up of problems may be of little lasting importance, but it is unpleasant at the time and must be borne somehow. It helped Carl to realize that the key to his bad day might lay in the feeling of shame he felt over what he did last evening. Whatever it was, he must have gone beyond what he himself could take comfortably. Once he recognized the limits his own conscience put on his conduct, he attempted to act accordingly and keep from further hurting himself and others.

Knowing what trips off such trying times is a first step in lessening their frequency and intensity. There may be a physical basis for some of these unhappy moods, especially during adolescence and menopause. There probably is an emotional element in these feelings of insecurity within oneself. As a person of any age faces new situations and attempts to undertake new roles, some ineffectiveness is inevitable. There may be a tendency to expect too much of oneself and of others that leaves a person disappointed with himself and discouraged with his relationships. This is why counseling is so often recommended for individuals who better want to cope with their concerns. Talking through one's moods and actions with a competent counselor gives an immediate relief from the tensions that build up inside. It also can provide an opportunity to develop insights as to why one acts as one does and of what one's day-to-day behavior means in terms of what one is trying to do. Once this step is taken, it is possible to find better means of handling one's frustrations.

Father's Work During the Teen Years

By the time a man has teenagers, he has been working long enough to know what his job entails. He has gotten along with difficult colleagues and handled the competition and conflict that is found in all working situations. He probably has enjoyed some aspects of his job and found others so irksome that he has considered shifting into another line of work at one time or another.

Making ends meet on his pay is apt to be a central concern now in the age of spiraling costs and high expenses at home. He may look for a second job, take overtime when he can get it, and worry about holding his present job when lay-offs are taking place. He may do what he can to hold down his expenses so that he can bring home more money to the household. Men sometimes take to carrying their lunch to save the time and money of eating out at noon. In some situations this deprives the man of needed contacts that are so important to his success. Car-pooling may ease the energy crisis and traffic on the highways, but it is not always feasible. Cutting travel and doing more business on the long distance telephone is a possibility some men find possible in reducing costs and having more time with the family. Entertaining more informally and less frequently is still another option to be considered. With financial pressures prodding him, he may or may not feel that this is a good time to change jobs or get into another line of work.

Retooling for a second career is a way out of a line of work where the future looks anything but promising. Seeing the writing on the wall, a man may opt for shifting into another line of work when the future of his present job looks dim. This may involve getting additional training for a different field or boning up in home study for a fresh start in more promising endeavors. It sometimes necessitates his being away from home more often and for more extended periods than have been necessary before. It takes cooperation on the part of his wife and children and some sacrifice on his part to effect the transfer.

Filling the roles of husband and father means walking a tightrope at times. The man of the house would like to wear the pants and act decisively, but he believes in the other members of his family having their say, too. He tries to be strong and firm, even when he needs comforting and solace himself. He realizes that his wife enjoys his romantic moods, but he is too busy and too tired to give her the loving attention she needs. He hears from his kids how other fathers behave and what they allow their children to do. He must make clear that there are standards that their family follows regardless of what other parents allow. He sees other husbands helping out at home more than he has time for and is made to feel a bit guilty when he appears to fall short of neighborhood expectations. Juggling all that is expected of him at home, at work, at church, and in his community connections takes some doing, and it is all too often the family that gets the short end of things. He knows this, but there seem to be few other options open to him.

Satisfying his own sense of who he is and what he wants to be and do can be all-pervasive during the years when there are teenagers in the home. There are so many other demands on his time and strength that he never has time for the fun and relaxation he most enjoys. He feels threats to his virility from images of masculinity on television and in his reading. His teenage sons challenge his strength and endurance with their newfound bravado. His teenage daughters and their girl friends tantalize him with the youth and beauty he longs for to bolster up his own failing self-image. He may assert himself and take up some of the interests that absorb his time and money. He may find his wife supporting his sagging vanity. He may enjoy his teenage children for the many things they can do together. Nevertheless, there are many moments when he wonders about himself and what life is all about where he is concerned.

Mother's Work—Here and There

That mother's work is never done is not always true of mothers of teenage sons and daughters. At times she is busy enough straightening the home after an invasion of teenagers, getting ready for a special function, or preparing the endless meals that her family requires. At other times, she feels useless. The teenagers are away from home at longer and longer intervals. Her husband is busier than ever, while she seems to be less needed than she has been since the children arrived years ago.

Should Mother get a job? This is a question that more families of teenagers consider than at any time of the family cycle since the children came. The family needs all the income it can get, and Mother is ready to find herself outside the home in many instances. She knows she will find even a part-time job rewarding, not only for the pay it will bring, but especially for the chance to get out among other people and to do something different. She probably left work when her first baby came and now is prepared to get back into the working force if the opportunity presents itself.

Before a woman goes to work outside her home, she and her family should do some careful calculating of what her employment will mean. Will her extra expenses and income taxes more than use up the money she gets? Will her time away from the family be a sacrifice for them and for her? Has she the strength, the talent, and the salable skills that will make her employment feasible? Can she get work at the level of her potential competence, or will she have to do something that is hardly worth her time? Who in the family will do some of the things around the home that will lighten her burden when she gets home from work?

Many parents feel that at least one of the parents should be at home when the children get home from school. This is true in many cases and not so imperative in others. Mother's working outside the home is not necessarily a hardship on her family. Studies have shown that mothers who have at least a part-time job may have a better relationship with their teenagers than do those who are full-time homemakers. The working mother is not so possessive of her young people and lets them make more of their own decisions. With mother at work, many a teenager assumes responsibilities for himself and his family that he has let mother do before. When mother is out among other people, she begins to appreciate her own children more than she has before. She gets a broader perspective of herself and them and finds letting them go and grow easier when she has some outside interests.

Some mothers have all they can do keeping up with their growing families. Some husbands will not consider their wives working. There are some professions where a wife is needed in supplemental ways to her husband's work. It all boils down to what makes sense for an individual family. Now that there are many options open for a woman and her family, it is theirs to choose as they see best.

Keeping romance in her marriage is hardly a task, but it is an ever-present challenge for the mother of teenage children. She tries to keep herself attractive for her mate and for her own feeling of self-worth. She does what she can to keep herself trim. She keeps her mind alert and growing in order to be an interesting companion for her husband and family, as well as to satisfy her own needs as a person. She is wise to keep alive some of her own central interests while her family is growing up so that she may continue to be a vital person.

She and her husband may sign up for one or more weekend retreats on how to enrich their marriage relationship now that the children are no longer young. They read about, discuss, and role-play some of the nuances in inter-play that are mutually satisfying. They sense that the children will not always be there with them and that their marriage is literally the foundation of the family now and in the future. So they do what they can to keep their marriage happy and satisfying.

Mother is the family's social director in most instances. She is the one through whom the couple's invitations and social plans are funnelled. She it is who entertains her friends, her husband's colleagues, her children's friends, and members of the family at regular intervals. She expects to write the birthday, anniversary, and holiday cards to near and dear ones. She keeps in touch with other members of the family by telephone, letter, and visiting. She tends to be the one who initiates special family trips and vacations and helps organize them once they have been undertaken. She may thoroughly enjoy these roles, or she may want her husband and older children to take over some of them as much as they can.

Sinking roots deep in faith and philosophy of life is one function of motherhood that cannot be ignored. For better or for worse, the basic stance of the family determines its well-being now and in the future. Religious families are more successful in raising their children successfully than are families with little or no religious ties. Mother usually takes the lead in church attendance and religious activities. Her husband and children may rail at her insistence on their participation but look to her for leadership in these things more often than not. This gives her and them the basic security they need in times of crisis and the vigor that their spiritual lives require.

Facing the Future Alone

More men and women whose children are teenagers face life without a marriage partner now than in previous times. Death, divorce, separation, either temporarily or permanently, leaves one parent to rear the children and cope with life alone. Now when so much is expected of marriage, more marriages are broken before the children are reared than once was the case. No one really wants a broken family, but they do occur and have to be cared for by the remaining parent.

Being both parents to the children is impossible. But many a mother does what she can to be both father and mother to her fatherless youngsters. This is hard when children are young. It is no less easy when they become teenagers who need a firm hand and a united front of both parents to set the limits they need. Yet, many a mother does astonishingly well in helping her teenagers find their own strengths in their father's absence. She risks needing them too much when they are all she has unless she is aware of the danger and ready to let them go without feeling guilty at abandoning her. She does this by seeing to it that she does not become entirely dependent upon her teenagers for the social and emotional support she needs as a person.

The father sometimes is the one left with children to raise after his wife has gone. He probably has some difficulty giving his daughters the womanly guidance they need, and so may call upon other women in the family, church, or neighborhood to play the roles that he cannot. He may have a fine relationship with his teenage sons or they may regret not being closer as a family. Each family is different in its membership, its attitudes, its problems, and its promises. Each must work out its own solutions to the problems that confront it.

Leading a normal social life is not easy for a single parent. He or she as a parent of teenagers is needed at home at the times when other adults are enjoying one another. Other men and women that the single parent knows go about as couples and make the single mother or father feel like a fifth wheel. The children may resist their mother's or father's dating, especially if they fear that it may become serious. It is generally agreed that the parent who faces the present and future alone should live as normally as possible. This is not easy without the cooperation of the older children, and the community at large.

Remarriage is a possibility fraught with problems. The man or woman or both may be wary of not making the same mistake twice. He or she may have few viable opportunities to meet and successfully win a compatible partner. Time available for the couple probably is curtailed by their family responsibilities. Even more serious is the resistance of teenage children to the courtship and marriage of their remaining parent.

Some teenagers are mature enough to want their mother or father to have a full adult life of his or her own. Unfortunately many teenagers resent the attention their parent pays to the new prospective member of the family. They become jealous of the attention paid to the other adult. They are afraid of what having a stepfather or stepmother will mean to them personally. They have had the single parent to themselves for long enough not to want any drastic changes in the family. So, they tend to make it difficult for the courtship or marriage to proceed as it otherwise might.

The parent left alone to rear the children has the alternative of living for the children and letting them dictate their preferences or making it clear that each must live his or her own life as seems best. This is a difficult choice. It is a rare parent who is willing to hurt the children, or to go against their wishes when they feel strongly about what affects them. It is a wise mother or father who can see beyond the teenagers' present resistance to the long pull of the future.

Parents Are People, Too

Each of the developmental tasks of parents of teenagers exacts its toll of patience and poise. If at times mother or father loses control, it can be taken in stride. Parents are human beings with all the foibles and frustrations, strengths and weaknesses, patience and impatience known to mankind. Each has a breaking point. Each can be pushed beyond the limit of his control. Parents need not be ashamed of their own honest feelings, even when they are annoyed, angry, or anxious to the point of panic.

Teenagers can learn to respect their parents as they are, without expecting them to be perfect all the time. Teenagers can do a great deal to ease the burdens their parents carry when the strain becomes apparent. Some sensitive teenage sons and daughters can express their affection for a vulnerable parent before the breaking point is reached.

Parents are trying to do a great many complicated things all at once in keeping the home going nicely, guiding their children, and maintaining their own best development as a couple and as individuals. If at times they seem trying to those who live with them, that is to be expected. Teenagers should be the first to recognize the signs of stress when an individual is pushed beyond his strength or confused about who he is and where he is going. This is something in common between parents and teenage sons and daughters that each can understand in the other.

6
Teen Troubles—Normal or Serious?

There is a danger in talking about teenagers' behavior. One becomes lost in generalizations about an entire age group. Whenever discussion begins, "Teenagers are . . . ," there is an implication that all teenagers feel, act, think, and relate in the same way. This, of course, is not true. Each teenager is most of all himself. He or she is still the boy or girl of the first ten or a dozen years of life. He or she is still the son or daughter of the family of which he has always been a part. Each has many of the same strengths and weaknesses, fears and hopes, sensitivities and feelings that characterized him during the years before the teens.

At the same time there are certain experiences and tendencies common to teenagers that persons in other age groups do not share to the same degree. There are some behavior patterns that are relatively normal in the teen years that might be construed as extreme in older people. Many parents become anxious about what their teenagers do. When their adolescents' behavior is potentially serious and when it is merely a passing phenomenon that will disappear as the young person matures is a distinction worth making. It provides some guidelines as to when to seek help for serious teenage problems and when to relax in confidence that the youngster is going through a phase that will pass in time.

Some Disrespect Is Normal

Few things irritate parents as much as teenagers' lack of respect. A father who is usually cool and assured in disciplining **75** his children loses his temper when his brash teenager defies him or is disrespectful to other adults. Even the most patient mother may lose control when her adolescent daughter is rude. When parents discuss what irritates them most in their teenagers' behavior, disrespect usually ranks high in their list of annoyances. Yet, some disrespect is normal and to be expected in the teen years.

Thrusts toward independence are rarely smooth and polite. A son or daughter must push away from family controls in order to become an independent person. It is not easy to loosen the ties of a lifetime between adolescent and parent. If the family has been a particularly close and loving one, the teenager's task of emancipation is apt to be even harder than it might be if his parents had always been more or less aloof and disinterested. The young person who has been especially close to his mother and father must take a stand that convinces his parents and himself that he is now his own person. This is done by a variety of behaviors that parents find distasteful, disrespectful, and distressing. But in a sense these unpleasant episodes are healthy and inevitable if the young person is to become fully mature.

Defiance can be deafening. Much adult criticism of teenagers centers in their noisiness. Neighbors complain about teenagers' raucous noise that disturbs their sleep. Motor bikes zoom, car brakes scream in the street. Loud talk and laughter as parties break up upsets the whole neighborhood.

Parents complain that their teenagers seem to turn them off as they turn up the volume of the stereo, radio, or television. "Turn that thing down" is an all too frequent command of parents who find ear-splitting the decibels that their teenagers enjoy. The modern music in fashion with teenagers has a beat that requires maximum volume, so the kids say. Besides, when they are listening to a favorite record or a popular group on radio or TV, they are beyond the beck and call of impatient parents. They are literally turned off to others around them, safe in an island of sound that defies intrusion.

One of the things that baffles adults is that teenagers can so often concentrate on their homework while listening to music that would be distracting to their elders. One explanation is that today's teenagers have grown up accustomed to loud sounds. Another is that adolescents unconsciously or deliberately use noise as a screen between themselves and others in order to concentrate on what they are doing.

Families make a variety of compromises in this area of conflict. Some insist that their teenagers use earphones when they listen to loud records or programs. Other parents provide space where their teenagers can make all the noise they want without disrupting the rest of the family. Still other households have established hours when reasonable noisiness is permitted and other quiet times when members of the family are resting, reading, or studying.

Privacy is worth fighting for in the family with teenagers. As a son or daughter becomes more and more himself or herself, there is a decided tendency to keep confidential aspects of life that parents may once have shared. This is a time when the bathroom door is locked against other family members. Teenagers need privacy for the personal grooming and self-inspection that leads to full acceptance and appreciation of their newly formed bodies. These are the days when a family need not worry if the teenager closes the door to his room. The understanding family recognizes that the young person needs privacy to study, to daydream, to arrange and rearrange his things, and to find himself or herself in a place to call his own.

It is an insult to a teenager to intrude in those parts of his or her life thought to be private and personal. Now, more than ever, a teenager's mail is to be respected as belonging to him alone. Even though the parents know from whom a letter may be and may already know much about its contents, it is the teenager himself to whom it is addressed who has the right to open and read it when and as he will. If the parents do not pry too much, their teenagers usually share such things in time.

When a parent or someone èlse reads a teenager's locked diary, it is distressing to any teenager. The purpose of a diary is to express one's innermost feelings and reactions to the experiences of life. It is meant for no other eyes. When parents, brothers or sisters, or others violate teenagers' trust by getting into their personal papers, they can expect a vigorous reaction. It is a wise family that respects the privacy of its members and sees to it that each child, adult, and teenager has the island of solitude needed for healthy growth.

Telephone talk becomes an issue in many a family with teenagers. The problem revolves both around the teenagers' right to talk in privacy to their friends and in their respect for the rights of others in the family to use the phone. When members of the family listen in on a teenagers' telephone call, they incur his or her displeasure. This can be a matter of conflict in the home, with the teenager insisting upon his or her right to use the phone without the interference of siblings or parents.

Parents find that teenagers' conversations over the telephone take an undue amount of time. It is not unusual for a teenager to engage in a long discussion with a friend only recently seen. This is hard for parents to accept, especially when they have urgent use of the family phone. From the teenager's point of view, it is the friend with whom he or she has been in intimate association with whom he can share impressions and get an evaluation of how the situation is going. Each one sees himself anew through his friends' eyes. During adolescence this is central in gaining a sense of one's own autonomy and personhood.

Families can arrange for both their teenagers and the others at home to use the telephone equitably. It is possible to limit the length of calls by the use of a timer by the telephone that signals the end of a call with a buzzer. Some families make it a rule not to allow telephoning during meal hours, so that the family may dine together in peace. Others give a priority to urgent professional and business calls so important to the working members of the family. This means that when Dad or Mother is expecting an important call, others in the family postpone their use of the phone until the awaited call has been completed. Some families can afford to give their teenagers their own telephone, thus relieving the pressure on the family phone. But even then there must be restrictions on expensive toll calls and excessive telephone bills. Each family must make its own arrangement for the use of its telephone in a way that respects the privacy of each of its members and provides a fair use of the phone by all.

Liking oneself as a teenager is an achievement. Even the most cocky-sounding young person has moments of self-doubt. This is a period when aspirations outdistance accomplishments, and what a teenager does is not what he or she was attempting. This is especially true in his or her relationships with other members of the family. The adolescent pushes off from parental control decisively, and may frighten himself with his impudence. Many a young fellow has crept back into the family circle with an open or implied apology after "telling off" one of his parents. His disrespect has made him ashamed of how he treated his mother or father, and so he does what he can to make amends.

Two steps forward and one back is a familiar pattern of conduct in teenagers. They insist upon their rights with disrespect if necessary to prove their point. They may rant and rave and make a scene to gain their independence. Then they regard their unpleasantness and do what they can to make amends. This results in two steps ahead toward autonomy followed by one step back into independence on the family once again. This is relatively normal behavior during the second decade of life, and nothing for either parents or their teenagers to worry about unduly.

Signs of Serious Teen Trouble

There are indications of distress in teenagers that alert adults can note. These are not the unpleasant, relatively normal types of conduct found in most adolescents. They are the symptoms of deeper trouble that bear watching and getting professional help for while there is yet time. Three syndromes of serious disturbance during the teen years are outlined below. Each of these is potentially dangerous enough to explore and treat as soon as possible. None is necessarily permanent but is probably more than a phase out of which a youngster will grow in time without help.

Violence and cruelty are signs of trouble in teenagers. The adolescent who is physically cruel to his pets or to other persons is showing signs of disturbance that should be taken seriously. Although many teenagers say cutting things to members of their families, they normally do not physically attack them. One who does is troubled beyond the normal limits. A teenager who is picked up for assault and battery should have something more than due process of law. He needs help to keep him from further developing a pattern of violence to others.

Rape is a serious offense that is damaging both to the girl and to the boy who sexually assaults her. It is not to be taken lightly nor sloughed off as anything the girl "asked for." Sex and violence are a dangerous combination that sometimes leads to murder and calls for professional examination and treatment.

Cruelty to pets and to children likewise is a symptom of distress calling for something more than punishment. When teenage Joanna battered the howling baby she was tending, her parents were aware that she needed help beyond anything the family could do for her. Any teenager can get upset when babysitting a child who will not quiet down. But to physically beat a baby is a serious thing not only for the infant but also for the individual who does the beating. This is conduct not limited to teenagers. Parents themselves have been known to beat their babies; they too need professional help.

Truancy and running away from home are calls for help. One of the first signs that a youngster is disturbed is his staying away from school. Many school children absent themselves from their classes from time to time. But any teenager who repeatedly stays away is consciously or unconsciously asking for help. Studies find that chronic truancy is a first step toward more serious difficulties. The teenager who stays out of school gets more and more deeply into trouble in an effort to hide his truancy and to keep himself occupied. It is important to find out why the teenager finds school so unsatisfactory. Sometimes it is a clash of personalities with a teacher or principal. It sometimes is a fear of failure or an indication of social maladjustment. Whatever the cause, it can be explored, and the young person can be helped to right himself before his problems become more critical.

Running away from home can be serious not only in the hazards that lie before a teenager but also in the problems that precipitated leaving home. A stepfather or mother whom a teenager cannot accept in the role of a parent may be the obvious reason for the runaway's taking off. Underneath, however, there may be an inability to cope with the new situation that calls for assistance. Teenagers have been known to run away from home for such reasons as a clash with mother or father, jealousy of a brother or sister, some intrusion on his privacy, or a desire for adventure and new experience. Any of these can be met by the family with less danger than the runaway may encounter in today's world.

Teenagers who hitchhike on the highways are asking for trouble. Many motorists are kind and considerate, but some are a threat to any young person they can lure into their automobiles. Young people adrift in any big city are easy prey for the most exploitive adult criminals. This is why police and other law enforcement officers are as alert as possible in finding and returning runaway teenagers to their families before they are molested, harmed, or worse. It is a wise family that can detect and meet a youngster's hunger for adventure *before* he or she takes off on his own. It is a loving family who welcomes a runaway teenager as the lost sheep who needs not so much punishment as loving care in order to find himself while there is still time.

Acting out behavior is a call for help. Those who work with disturbed youth see repeated and excessive drinking, drug usage, sex jams, and reckless driving as "acting out" efforts to get the help they need with their lives. Many teenagers have occasional episodes of irresponsibility. They go along with other young people in smoking pot, drinking alcoholic beverages, driving "like crazy," and otherwise "acting smart." Usually these are experimental and temporary lapses in more responsible behavior. They may be considered efforts of a youngster to prove himself and to challenge adult rules or to follow models other than those of his parents. If the teenager is not too hurt by the results of such experiments in living dangerously, he or she may be expected to mature along more socially accepted lines.

When an adolescent or young adult repeatedly goes in for excesses he or she may be seen as looking for something that is missing in life. That something sometimes is a lack of a sense of worth in himself. It often is an active repudiation of too severely strait-laced family patterns. It may be a desire for punishment for some misdeed the young individual has not been able to live with in himself.

Withdrawing from others for long periods of time is a sign of trouble in a teenager. All young people have a need for occasional intervals of isolation. They all desire seclusion at times to work through their problems and come to terms with themselves. But when a young person's withdrawal from normal social and family life goes on for an extended period of time, it is a sign of real distress.

Arthur had gradually removed himself from association with friends, classmates, and his family over the past several months. He had taken to his room, kept his door locked, and allowed no one to come in to see him. His mother left his meals outside his door and found evidence that he prowled the house and yard at night when the other members of the family were asleep. His rabbits in hutches adjoining the garage continued to get his conscientious care as the only living creatures with whom he maintained contact.

His doctor made the rabbits a point of contact that was to open the door to Arthur's room, and to his problem. One of the prize female rabbits had been bred, and as she neared her term, she was obviously in trouble. Arthur delayed getting the veterinarian for her and that night found her dead in her hutch. His mother heard him sobbing in his room early that morning, and had her first conversation with him in weeks through the door to his room. She called the family doctor who came out to the house before breakfast and did an autopsy on the boy's pet rabbit. The doctor found six dead rabbit fetuses within an obstructed birth channel.

Arthur came out to join the doctor, and in his grief poured out his own unhappy story. He had been in a deep depression over many months. It had been brought on originally by a severe case of acne that covered his face and neck until he was ashamed to go out in public. As he withdrew further into himself and isolated himself from all others, he became so depressed that he was incapable of acting in his own behalf. It was not until he lost his prize rabbit that he became available for the professional help he so urgently needed.

Arthur responded well to treatment and within the following year had finished high school. Arthur's story might not have ended so happily had not his mother called the doctor to help him that early morning or if the physician had been less perceptive of the boy's serious emotional illness. Parents do not hesitate to call the doctor when a youngster has a physical ailment. But all too often they delay in getting help for a teenager's mental and emotional illness, until he, and they, have lost valuable time.

Finding Help When It Is Needed

There is a tendency to delay getting outside help for teenagers' problems. Parents tend to hope that the youngster will outgrow his difficulties in time. Of course, many young people do, but many others are irreparably hurt for want of help they urgently need. Fathers and mothers are reluctant to admit that their attention is no longer enough to take care of their children's distress. This is especially true of emotional illness. Father may urge his son or daughter "to snap out of it." Mother may feel that if the youngster really wanted to improve he would. Parents find it hard to know when to seek help and when to relax and let time work its cure.

When to get help for adolescents' problems can be outlined fairly well. Before the trouble becomes critical or chronic is the general rule. This is all very well as a general principle. But how is a parent to know when a problem is becoming chronic? Who is to say when a teenager's distress will become critical? These are technical questions that baffle even the expert and are quite beyond the average parent's comprehension.

Parents and teenagers are wise to get help when they find themselves preoccupied with their current problems. Anything that is disturbing enough to keep you awake at night can be seen as appropriate for outside help. This is especially true when your thoughts about the problem seem to go around and around without getting anywhere. Usually when confronted with a dilemma, a teenager or his parents can see what the trouble is and take steps to correct it. But at times a problem is so baffling that thinking becomes circular and the family seems unable to get anywhere in solving it. Then some outside source may be most helpful in getting off dead center and making progress again.

Anything that sets off bad dreams, gives you recurrent nightmares, and is obviously deeply upsetting to you should be taken seriously. This is as true for parents as for their teenagers. When a member of either generation is undergoing strain that disturbs normal sleep and dream patterns, it is time to go for help. Talking out the problem that disturbs you ventilates the inner anguish and clarifies the nature of the distress. Getting at the root of the difficulty opens the way to considering ways out of the tangle. With professional help, almost any personal or family burden can be lightened, both for the parents and for their teenagers. What helps members of the one generation usually relieves the distress in the other.

Who needs help—the parents or the teenager? It is simple to respond that they probably both do. When something is deeply disturbing to a teenager, his parents feel it, too. When anything upsets the parents, the teenager's life reflects it. In an association as intimate as family life, what affects one member touches the others as well. This is particularly true of those relationships in which one person feels responsible for the other, as in marriage and family life.

The person who first sees the need for treatment is the one to go for help, regardless of who is in deepest need of it. Marriage counselors find that it is often the healthier member of the couple who comes first for marriage guidance. As he, or more often she, gets new insight into the marriage, his behavior is modified, and the other member of the pair becomes more available. So too, with parent-teenager relationships, the individual most ready for helpful discussion of the problem is the one to seek it out. As he or she becomes more understanding of himself and of the nature of the relationships that disturb him, he becomes easier to live with, and the other family members respond in more appropriate ways.

Where teenagers turn for help varies greatly. Some young people have the kind of mutually open relationship with their parents that allows them to discuss almost anything, at any time. But this is rare, and it almost never is all that a young person needs in adult guidance. The major reason is that the teen years are the time when a youngster must stretch away from his parents far enough to find out how other adults feel about some of the issues and values of life. So, even when the parent-teenager relationship is unusually open, the teenager needs other adults to consult, at times.

Some junior and senior high schools have excellent guidance staff members who are available to discuss anything that concerns their students. They see themselves as concerned with more than the academic progress of the young people in the school. They welcome any boy or girl who wants to explore any area of life that concerns them. Their counseling is confidential so that the young person need have no fear that what he says will get out to others without his express permission. Most school counselors these days have had special training and experience in personal guidance and are generally competent to help teenagers with their problems.

A favorite teacher may be a teenager's first choice for a confidential chat. Some teachers and students have especially good rapport so that it is easier to talk about things that concern them than it would be to go to someone not as well known or liked. Teachers of such courses as home economics, science, or shop in which laboratory work takes up several hours a week get especially well acquainted with their students in informal settings conducive to personal interaction.

A church school teacher, youth leader, or minister may be the person a teenager chooses to confide in when he faces problems beyond his ability. Church staff members are not equally qualified to counsel young people. A given teenager would be reluctant to talk over personal problems with one such adult, but find another easy to relate to in confidential ways. It boils down to whomever the teenager feels comfortable enough with to open up the situations that are distressing at the time. A religious leader should be aware of the depth and scope of young people's problems enough to refer to other more qualified professionals problems beyond his competence. Some city churches have consulting psychologists and psychiatrists available for consultation and referral in cases where more extensive or intensive treatment is indicated.

Parents tend to turn for help to members of their family, to their pastor, and to their family doctor. Any of these may be a good first step to solving the problem at hand. The family member, pastor, or physician may be all that is required to handle a relatively usual problem of a normal adolescent.

When deeper illnesses are involved, the nearby person consulted is wise to encourage the troubled family member to consult more expert sources.

Guidance clinics, mental health services, and family counseling centers are available in some cities and counties. These are usually staffed by competent professional persons who can diagnose and treat the usual problems that teenagers and their parents present. They generally have available for consultation and referral adjunct psychiatrists and other specialists for more involved and complicated causes. These modern resources are to be recommended over the older home-remedy-type of approach to human tangles. They save time and emotional energy in the long run and can be counted on for competent help when anything less is not enough.

Since most such services are supported by public and private funding, they are not excessively expensive. They usually charge fees appropriate for the family's ability to pay in amounts discussed early in the contact, so that there is no worry about how much the service is to cost. A family that would not hesitate to lay out several thousand dollars to straighten its children's teeth, should be quite as willing to pay what is necessary to keep a teenager's mind and spirit healthy. Attitudes about getting help for personal problems are changing these days to the place where most families consult outsiders from time to time during the turbulent period when there are teenagers in the home. This is as it should be. There need be no shame or guilt in going for help when it is needed.

7
Pressures to Conform

As long as sons and daughters conform to their parents' wishes and expectations, there is usually no problem at home. The two generations concur on most things and are happy with one another. The children follow their parents' advice and obey most of the time. But the time comes when older children and adolescents no longer look only to their parents for guidance. They are influenced more and more by other young people outside the family. Then Mother and Father become concerned about the pressures to conform that their children confront outside the family.

Conformity Thrusts in the Teens

Step into almost any high school across the country and you note at once how alike the students appear to be. They wear the same type of clothing, adopt similar posture and stance, effect identical hairstyles, repeat the same words and slogans, and do everything possible to appear as though they have been poured out of the same mold. In their efforts to emancipate themselves from their parents, teenagers get locked into even greater restrictions in the demands of their peers. Let some luckless youngster step out of the narrow path that others follow and he or she is pushed back into line with such powerful methods as name-calling, ridicule, sarcasm, and outright snubbing.

Do their friends lead them astray? Many a parent comes to the conclusion that it is the bad company their teenagers **88** keep that gets them into trouble. This is especially true of the adolescent boys who get into trouble of one kind or another. A family therapist who works with delinquent youth reported that some boys reject the values, standards, and discipline of the parents often in the name of freedom, and unwittingly become slaves and captives to the mores and discipline of the gang. Rather than weighing the statements of the parents against the statements of their peer groups and then objectively deciding in which direction they will go, some boys go in the direction their gang indicates almost by reflex action.

The urge to rebel is encouraged by the boy's pals, but it originates within the lad himself. He conforms to his gang as a way out of his family's sphere of influence. That he gets even more deeply into a new and more dangerous kind of dependence—on the gang—he does not bargain for. He is in the midst of a lunge out of his boyhood and toward manhood that does not provide the objectivity or the calmness it would take to foresee all the dangers of going along with the other young rebels around him.

"Don't tell me what to do" is heard in many a family with teenagers. They listen to anything some pimply-faced boy tells them but turn a deaf ear to their parents. A story that is making the rounds of one suburban community goes this way:

Teenager: "I'm off to the party now."

Parents: "Have a good time."

Teenager: "Don't tell me what to do!"

Silly as it sounds, it rings in many a family setting, even if the words are not said. The dynamics of turning to the peer group rather than to the parents during the teen years is a normal and to be expected characteristic of adolescence.

What the other kids say is important to teenagers. They want desperately to be accepted by their peers. They long to be acceptable to the other girls and fellows of their own age. They need young friends, and they know it. They have to feel that they are part of the young generation in obvious ways. They do all they can to look like others of their age. They try to sound like each other. They imitate the behavior of one another and of the young people slightly older than they are. They find themselves under a great deal of pressure to go to the functions that are "in" at the moment. Many of them feel so intensely about following the crowd that they will do almost anything to keep in its good graces.

"Nobody does that anymore" is avoided at all costs by teenagers. What was all the rage when parents were young is ridiculously old-fashioned now. Styles in dress, grooming, speech, and behavior that were quite acceptable one or two student generations ago now are passé. The pressure is to go along with whatever the leaders of the present generation dictate if at all possible. The pacesetters of the younger generation cannot be expected to follow the family's values. Their very appeal is to challenge its authority in every way they can. The pressure to repudiate parents, teachers, ministers, and the responsible institutions they represent takes many forms. What most adults see as undesirable types of teenage behavior are overt acts of rebellion against "the establishment." Of course this upsets parents—it is supposed to!

Parents do not need to knuckle under pressures that threaten their children's well-being. They can stand up and insist that their own teenagers avoid the dangerous practices that lure them into trouble. They have the right and the responsibility to set limits beyond which their sons and daughters are not allowed to go. This is important for their teenagers who must feel some boundaries for their behavior in order to be free within them. It is essential for the parents' sense of responsibility to keep their children from crashing on the shoals of heedless youth. Wise parents, therefore, give their teenagers freedom within necessary limits.

Pressures on Parents to Conform

Parents feel undue pressure to go along with what others dictate during the years that they have teenage children at home. Their own teenagers make demands upon them that are loud and clear. They are called out-of-date and "not with it" by their modern youngsters. They are told that "all the other kids are . . ." so often that they begin to wonder if it is true that their sons and daughters are being held back by their family's modest expectations.

"All the other kids" is a powerful myth. Powerful because so many teenagers are so swayed by it. Mythical because there are very few things that all other young people do, say, or feel, however it appears to any given young person. "Everybody else" usually refers not to all the young people in the community, to the whole student body, or even to all of one's agemates in a class. "All the other kids" are those in the particular group that a teenager looks to as models at the moment. They probably are generally accepted leaders in the local situation at the time. They possibly are the group your teenager would like to be a part of if possible. Challenge any teenager who quotes "all the other kids" to name two, and you may get a clue as to the leader or leaders your youngster is trying to emulate. The chances are that such influential members of your teenager's generation are not advocating the conduct you value most highly. Their very appeal is that they differ from what parents generally are and would have their teenagers become.

Other parents and neighbors exert powerful pressures upon parents. Mr. and Mrs. Jones feel that keeping in touch with their children's teachers and schooling is important. That was all very well during the youngsters' early school experience. But once their sons and daughters got into junior and senior high school it became increasingly difficult. Their children no longer welcomed their visits to school. Other parents joined the youngsters in taking a "hands off" stance during the secondary school period. The PTA, once a good way for parents and teachers to know one another, dwindled after the seventh grade to the place where the Joneses felt they were carrying it all by themselves. They gradually yielded to pressure to disband even though they both felt that it was still important and should be continued.

Some parents initiate social life for their teenagers that is hard for other mothers and fathers to accept. It is not unusual for some mothers to push their daughters into sophisticated social affairs beyond the readiness of many of the other girls their age. They give elaborate parties that cannot be reciprocated easily. They allow their daughters to wear clothing other mothers feel are more suitable for much older girls. They serve spiked punch and turn a blind eye to what goes on at teenage functions. They encourage pairing off at early ages and fail to give the kind of supervision of boy-girl parties that other parents feel is necessary. Those parents who do not approve of such premature pushing of young people into artificial social situations find it hard to resist. They may fear getting the reputation of being old-fashioned, goody-goody, or "not with it." They are reminded by their teenagers of what other mothers permit and are made to feel that they are not keeping up with the times. They risk losing their teenagers and their friends if they are too strict in limiting their hospitality.

Gretchen made a scene when her parents insisted on remaining at home when she gave her first boy-girl party. The next door neighbors had invited Gretchen's parents over to their house for the evening when they heard of her party. They assumed, of course, that Gretchen's parents would not want to interfere with the young people that evening. Gretchen thought their invitation to her parents was a fine idea and could not understand her mother's refusal. Gretchen's father tried to explain that they were staying home that evening not to "snoopervize" but to be on hand as senior hosts, should they be needed. As it turned out, they were justified in their decision. When several older, uninvited boys crashed the party, Gretchen needed her father's firm hand to control the situation. But until that time Gretchen's parents felt as though they were defying neighborhood customs, and going against the pressure of other adults as well as the kids.

Society restricts adults in many ways. There are countless rules, regulations, customs, and expectations that parents confront as pressures on their lives. Some of these pressures are in the form of laws protecting the community at large. Others are necessary in order to maintain one's status and standard of living. Still others are required if one is to be well-thought-of in the neighborhood. Many are supposedly discretionary but actually are backed up with a great deal of community pressure. Parents of teenagers feel all of these pressures and restrictions that other adults do. And, in addition they are pushed into situations they would like to avoid by their teenagers and the other adults around them. Standing firm and holding to their convictions, while remaining open and flexible as parents, demands agility beyond anything required before. It is a sturdy parent who can live under such pressure. It is a wise parent who can help teenagers see that they are not the only ones who must cope with others' demands, that this indeed is a part of becoming an adult in interaction with other adults.

Nonconforming Individuals

There are many individuals of all generations who do not fit the mold. They live their own lives without too much worry about what other people think. Some of these are so atypical they are locked up, or live outside the law, always on the run, trying to keep from getting caught for something society does not permit its members. Some are ostracized and shunned for not conforming to what is expected. Some live in isolated communities with others of their kind where they make their own rules and live according to their beliefs. Others are exceptional in some degree that makes them different and set apart from others in one or more ways.

Gifted, talented individuals may be persons apart. The musical genius does not play ball with the other fellows for fear he might hurt his hands so necessary for his practicing. He keeps to himself and his instrument rather than hanging out with the other teenagers. He composes a concerto rather than taking a girl to the movies. His parents may be proud of his talent and yet wish that he could be more like other young people. So it is with the intellectually gifted who keeps to his books. The young philosopher who prefers the company of the old professor to that of "silly kids" his age baffles his parents at the same time that they admire his deep thinking. The teenage scientist who spends her last dollar for the microscope she needs instead of for the party dress she does not want puzzles her father and makes her mother wonder if she will ever live as other girls do. It takes a special kind of parental appreciation to let a teenager do his own thing when it differs from what other young people are doing.

Handicapped, limited teenagers have special problems that require special opportunities and understanding. The young person confined to a wheelchair cannot do many of the things that more mobile teenagers take for granted. If he is overly protected, he may become even more dependent. As long as his spirit soars and his mind remains alert, he can enter into many of the activities and enjoy most of the interests of other teenagers his age. He is crippled indeed if he is not given the chance to do and be what he can.

Quiet, contemplative teenagers march to a different drum. For one reason or many, they do not conform to the usual teenage behavior. Their parents may do their best to "get them out of themselves" only to find that their efforts result in more withdrawal. Too shy to enter into teenage activities around them, they set their parents to worrying about what is wrong and how they can be helped. Mothers feel the pressure of other mothers whose daughters are popular. Fathers smart under the man-talk in the neighborhood that so often centers in their sons' prowess in sports and other masculine activities. It takes patience on the part of both parents to accept, in the face of neighborhood pressures, their sons and daughters as they are.

Teenagers in the drug scene are a problem to themselves and others. They take up drugs as an escape from current reality, and often run amuck of the law. Their parents hesitate to restrict them for fear they will get even further into trouble. They sometimes blame their parents for their drug-usage by citing the pills in the family medicine chest. Young drug users excuse themselves by reporting their parents' rejection or neglect as the reason for their turning on. This adds to their parents' pain and postpones the teenagers' assumption of responsibility for his or her own behavior.

Every teenager is unusual in some sense. Each has his or her own promise and potential. Each has his or her own bent and interests, hopes and aspirations, frustrations and problems. No one is like any other in any but a few outward characteristics. This makes difficult the teenager's problem of establishing a clear sense of personal identity. It is a continuing challenge of parents to keep closely enough in touch with their growing youth to give them the encouragement and opportunities for finding themselves they need.

Conformity Is on the Surface

Pressures to conform are greatest in the superficial areas of life. This is found throughout society. Families feel the pressure to "keep up with the Joneses" in the kind of house they live in, in the type of cars they drive, the clothes they wear, and the way they act in public. At home a family is free to be itself. It values its privacy as a way of protecting those aspects of life that are truly its own. So it is with much of the conformity pressures upon youth.

Teenagers follow the crowd in ways that show they are with it. Studies find that conformity to group norms among teenagers is most conspicuous in obvious characteristics. They enjoy the same idioms of speech that may be baffling to their elders—that is part of their charm! Teenagers often talk big to hide their inexperience. They use wry humor to mask their embarrassment in many a social situation. They take to puns as a way of appearing at home in the group that may make them uneasy in one or more ways. The result is to sound like other young people, as much as possible, without risking what one is and is trying to become.

Superficial characteristics are easily changed. It takes but a few minutes to change one's hairstyle, adopt other speech patterns, or to quit "horsing around." All it takes in most instances is the disapproval of someone whom one admires to effect a complete turn-about. Let a new girl friend comment upon a boy's obesity, and he goes on a diet that amazes his family. Let a favorite teacher express confidence in a girl's ability to express herself appropriately, and her poor punning gives way to more mature ways of speaking. Youngsters who have "clowned around" in junior high school are more reserved when they find themselves in the sober setting of the big consolidated high school in the next town. So, too, when young people go to college, their former behavior drops away, and they soon reflect the image of the campus.

Public behavior shifts with the setting and the time. The same young people in blue jeans and sneakers on a work project Saturday morning are quite a different crowd when dressed for the prom that evening. In the morning their public behavior is loud, jocular, informal, and active. The evening finds them more quietly minding their manners and acting in ways appropriate to their dress and to the setting in which they are. They behave differently in a mixed group than when the girls are alone or the boys are by themselves. This is true of adults as well. Each generation and every society has complex patterns of behavior appropriate to various situations. These must be learned if a person is to be accepted. They are not to be confused with the private life of the individual. That is more deeply imbedded, more permanent, and more revealing of the real person than is the "front" behind which he appears in public.

Parents Influence Teenagers

More than most teenagers admit, they are influenced by their parents. More than many parents realize, they are still the most important people in their teenage children's lives.

Even the most rebellious appearing young person is still his father's child, and he knows it—that may be what upsets him at the moment. Teenagers follow, as they must, the other kids of their own age in many of the overt ways of looking and behaving. But in most of the things that really count they look to their parents.

Research finds teenagers follow their families in areas of major importance. Studies over recent decades indicate clearly that teenagers tend to continue family patterns in significant ways. If parents value education, their sons and daughters tend to go farther in their schooling than those of less well-educated fathers and mothers. When a family is devoted to art, music, science, or religion, its children tend to be interested in the same or similar areas.

Vocations run in families significantly more often than not. A boy may rebel from his father's pressure to go into the family business, only to find a place for himself in something remarkably similar in time. A girl may vow that she will never work as hard as her mother, only to get into much the same occupational and community interests that have kept her mother so involved through the years.

Personal practices are homemade. Habits of neatness or sloppiness tend eventually to go from generation to generation. Through the teen years there may be a mild revolt from parental expectations of a semblance of orderliness, but eventually the family habits win over. Studies show that teenagers who drink tend to have parents who enjoy their liquor, while teenagers who do not have families who refrain. Smoking runs in families as the children learn early to take to what their parents do or do not do. It is an unusual teenager who never on any occasion has had a drink or tried to smoke. These experiments are usually brief and transitory efforts to stretch away from stricter family standards that tend eventually to prevail.

Repudiation of family practices does happen. The overwhelming tendency of a family's children is to reproduce the family patterns in most major areas of life. But there are exceptions. When a family is unduly harsh and rigid in bringing up its children, the children may revolt and do exactly the opposite in one or more ways. When children feel that they are not favored or given the loving attention they need, they may repudiate their parents by taking on entirely different life-styles. The alcoholic's son never touches the stuff. The seductive mother's daughter becomes Miss Prim-and-Proper. The penurious family brings up a youngster who spends every dollar he gets as soon as he gets it. The tendency is for children to do as the family does in ways that are healthy and fulfilling and to refrain from following the family in areas where the child has been unduly hurt. The relatively happy family that has reared its children within an atmosphere of love and mutual caring more often than not has sons and daughters who carry on that tradition.

Teenagers rate their parents highly. This may appear like the overstatement of the year. But when social scientists asked high school students to rate both themselves and their parents on a number of areas of interest to them, they found that parents outranked teenagers in the minds of most of the students. Even the cockiest adolescent admits at times that his parents are wiser than he. In fact, the more highly a youngster values his parents' judgment, the more vehemently he rebels from it when he has to assert himself. In a sense, adolescent rebellion is as much from the young person's dependence on his parents as it is from the parents themselves.

Grace left the table with her black eyes flashing. Her comment hurled at her mother as she slammed the door was a revealing: "I know you know what I should do. But I have to be right sometimes, and even if I'm not I have to try my own way." This sums up the teenage-parent dilemma well. Even when young people recognize that their parents know what is best for them, they must make up their own minds and do things the way they want to, even when they make mistakes. Fortunately, most teenagers learn from their mistakes and come eventually to a place not far from where their parents have been guiding them.

Teen Pressures Ease in Time

The sense of urgency with which many teenagers follow the dictates of the crowd tapers off as adolescence continues. What begins in the grade-school years when some boys and girls turn to their peers and away from their parents as influential guides of their lives, reaches a peak during the adolescence and has but modest impact in the later teens.

The early and middle teen years are marked by high conformity to peers and criticism of adults. Studies have found that as young teenagers find themselves as a group, they become critical of the things around them. They complain about the shabbiness of the school, the church, and their homes. They give the impression that the adults around them have provided poorly for them and that they could do a much better job of it themselves. This gives sensitive adults a clue as to how to handle what otherwise is a difficult stage. Families that encourage their adolescent sons and daughters to take the initiative in redoing their rooms, helping plan family redecorating, and exploring ways of brightening the home often find the youngster eager, willing, and competent. As they gain experience their appreciation for the complexities of what seemed simple at first increase, and they see more of what their parents have been up against all along.

By the middle teens criticism of parents and other adults peaks. Research reports that at sixteen a girl is apt to be more critical of her mother than she has been before or will be again. She criticizes her mother's housekeeping and the way she rears the children. She seems sure that she could do these things far better than her mother is doing them. She gets reinforcement from her girl friends which gives her the courage to compare her mother unfavorably with other females in appearance, grooming, and personal conduct. It is at this point that many a mother is moved to exasperation. If she can see what is happening from the girl's point of view, she has a head start on meeting the situation.

Sixteen-year-old Belle fussed at her mother for not doing her hair as fashionably as did the mothers of some of her girl friends. Mother responded that she would be happy to have Belle give her some advice on the hairstyling that she had in mind. Belle was delighted. She shampooed and redid her mother's hair in a way that pleased them both. In the process the two women got into a confidential chat that was warmer and more intimate than the two had had for some time. The girl friends approved the new coiffure, and what might have been a conflict of conformity ended in a meeting of minds.

By the late teen years, most young people have had enough success in finding themselves that they do not need such close adherence to the norms of their peers. They usually have come through the roughest of the period of emancipation from their parents and are able to relate on a more mature basis. The late adolescent and young adult can now be interdependent both in receiving and in giving help. They now can risk being more openly appreciative of their families. This is especially true when they get a great deal of emotional support and warmth from their parents.

Love them and let them go is a simple recommendation for parents whose teenagers avidly conform to youth their own age and reject much their family expects. Parents can hold their children only with open hands. They must be prepared to release their teenagers in order for the young to attain adulthood. This does not mean turning a cold shoulder upon them. Rather it calls for a great deal of love to let a youngster make his own mistakes and to learn from them. As budding young adults feel the warm support of their parents behind them they can leave their childish ways with their family's blessing. Now they no longer have to look to their peers for courage to be. It bubbles up from within with life-affirming exuberance.

8
Teens' Best Friends

Best friends mean a great deal to teenagers. They give a feeling of belonging so important to young people in the second decade of life. They serve as confidants with whom can be shared the anxieties, disappointments, and insecurities of the teen years. They mutually support one another under stress and strain, and they rejoice with another when things go well. Both girl and boy friends are a part of growing into full maturity. Each can provide the experience of loving and being loved by persons outside the family so essential for entering the adult world.

Parents Have Mixed Feelings About Boy-Girl Friends

Parents do not always share their teenagers' enthusiasms for their best-friend-of-the-moment. The more intense the feeling their son or daughter has for some special person, the more concerned the parents are apt to be. They have a hard time letting their offspring go to other associations that may not seem worthy of them. Parents are partial to their own children. It is not unusual for a mother or a father to feel that their children's best friend is not good enough for him or her. It is not difficult to find some fault with the other young person, his family, or his conduct. So, parents are tempted to be overly critical of the special friends whom their children greatly value.

Parents fear premature involvement. They do not want their young people to be swept off their feet by feelings too strong to control. The more intense the teenager's feeling for the **101** sweetheart of the moment, the more concerned the parents are. The parents are afraid that their budding young adults will get involved in emotional tangles that will disrupt their studies. They do not want to see their sons or daughters hurt by too early love affairs. They know all too well how painful unrequited love can be. They would like to protect their children from being jilted and cast aside. They sense how easy it is for young people, inexperienced in the ways of a man with a maid, to give too much too soon. They know how often this results in being left with nothing but regret and a little packet of mementoes. They would like to protect their young-sters from life, but they know this is impossible, so they feel ineffectual as parents up against powerful forces over which they have little control.

Parents want their children to be popular. Mothers take pride in their teenagers' evidence of being liked by boys and girls their own age. They tell other mothers about the invitations their sons and daughters receive. They get satisfaction in know-ing that they have raised their children to be socially accept-able to others. They find vicarious pleasure in their young people's social life. They remember the joy they knew when their friends and they were young. Now, as parents, they would like their teenagers to enjoy their youth without some of the pain that so often comes with it. They try to be helpful in guiding their children's friendships, but all too often their experience is out-of-date as their teenagers see it. So parents tend to feel out of their children's lives just when they would most like to be included.

"They don't do that anymore" is what adults hear from today's young people. The formal courting grandparents talk about seems antiquated to young moderns. Dating their parents did a generation ago is no longer the same. Relationships between teenage boys and girls are more informal now. Their fun is usually as casual as their clothes. Males and females now more often look alike, sound similar, and do many of the same things in much the same way. Their conduct is more

reciprocal now than once was considered proper. Either the boy or the girl can initiate an activity in sports, music, drama, study, or service project that they work on together. This makes for less posing among friends and for an easier transition into the young adult social world.

Friends of the Same Sex

Parents, who are so often anxious about too early boy-girl friendships, tend to worry when their boy or girl shows little interest in the other sex. When a teenager reaches the teens without much mixed-group activities, the family may fear that something is the trouble. They like to feel that their children are perfectly normal and are developing in wholesome ways.

Best friends of the same sex are a natural part of adolescence. Boys like to get together for some of the boy-talk that is so important for them as budding young men. Girls confide in one another things of special interest to females. All are drawn to other persons of their own sex who share similar interests and have skills in the same things. While both sexes enjoy many things together, there are some things that can be best shared with a member of one's own sex. This does not mean that a teenager has homosexual tendencies. After a particularly intense friendship with some special pal, most young people proceed to relationships with members of the other sex that may be quite as meaningful while they last. The teen years are characterized by a variety of friends any of whom may be especially close at one time or another. Even when a young person is deeply wounded in some relationship, he learns from each person he knows and loves and matures through the experience each provides.

Scars from past experience take a time to get over. A girl who has been humiliated by some boy or man can be so deeply hurt that she avoids all males for a while. Abigail is a case in point. As an early teenager she was madly in love with a somewhat older boy who gave her the attention she craved. He acted as though he loved her and led her into intimacies she had never known before. After a few passionate weeks, he took off leaving Abby feeling jilted and abused. It was several years before she could trust a boy again. It took good old Joe whom she had known as a neighbor for years to help her overcome her fear of fellows. In time she could relax and enjoy members of the other sex, as other girls did. Her early experience temporarily slowed her development of friendships with boys until she could work through her distrust of them.

Boys, too, can be rebuffed by females to the place where they retreat into all-male companionship for awhile. Andy had a terrific crush on a young teacher's aid several years his senior when he was still in junior high. Instead of treating his feelings with mature understanding and gentleness, she put him up to public ridicule that cut him to the quick. He dropped out of her class from that day forward and refused to talk about the incident, even to clear his academic record. It was not until Andy got into senior high that he recovered sufficiently from this early pain at the hands of a woman to be able to relax and enjoy girls again.

Absorbing interests can delay boy-girl friendships. While two boys are remodeling the second-hand car they jointly bought, they have no time for girls and other interests. They are completely wrapped up in finding spare parts, cleaning, and putting together their precious automobile. Girls caught up in the enthusiasm of training to be junior counselors at a girls' camp or to become junior volunteers at the local hospital temporarily drop out of mixed-group functions. Invitations that once would have thrilled them now are turned down because they are just too busy. Teenagers who throw themselves into such absorbing interests as music, writing, drama, science, religious renewal, public speaking, or readying themselves for college forego some of their social activities for awhile. Once their objective has been attained, or is in sight, and they know the flush of success, they can go on to the boy-girl friendships that have been there potentially all along.

Friends of the same sex are safer for awhile. The teenager who has long-term goals that call for intense application for years may deliberately postpone intense heterosexual friendships until he or she is ready to be emotionally involved. Professions like medicine, law, the ministry, physics, or diplomacy are demanding in their training. Any teenager is wise to keep from any of the entangling alliances that would endanger the future prospects of such an occupation. As he or she nears the completion of the long period of preparation, there is time enough to become interested in members of the other sex. There are problems in such a course. By the time the young doctor or lawyer has finished his professional education, many likely prospects for marriage have been passed over. Then too, in giving himself or herself so completely to the pursuit of a career, the development of social skills has been postponed. So, when the young person at last turns to the opposite sex, he does not know how to handle such a friendship as smoothly as others in the picture.

What Does It Take to Be Popular?

Most young teenagers wonder how they can best get members of the other sex to take notice of them. They see other teenagers getting along smoothly with one another and yearn to have friends of both sexes who like them, too. Some foolishly go in for way-out behavior that defeats their purpose. Others pretend not to be interested or to be so busy they have no time for frivolity. Actually most young people want friends, and they know it. They must all learn for themselves how to win friends and enjoy others.

Social competence is learned. The ability to get others' attention and to develop friendships is learned in action. No one is born popular. Each must learn how to introduce oneself into a group, how to be an interesting conversationalist, how to become a valued companion, how to heal the hurts of social interaction,—how to mature out of personal experience with a wide variety of human beings of both sexes.

Teenagers who have grown up in socially active families

have an inside track in developing social skills. They early learned how to handle social situations of many kinds. They go out in friendly ways to other people with the smiling reassurance that makes them approachable. They have learned the rudiments of courtesy and custom from early childhood onward. They know how to talk and to listen so that there is real interaction in their contacts with one another. They may seem to be "just naturally popular." But their secret is not in anything they were born with; they simply have had the experience of social interchange through the years that has made them effective with other people.

Specific skills are social assets. When our own daughters were young teenagers, they discovered that it is the girl who can do things who goes places. Know how to swim, and you get invited to pool and beach parties. Be a good sailor, and you get to serve as crew on boat rides. Play an acceptable game of tennis, golf, or bridge, and you are sought after to make up a foursome. Know how to bowl or play Ping-Pong, and the teenagers who want a game think of you. Know something about baseball, football, hockey, or basketball, and you get invited to the games. The teen years are a good time to learn as many of the games and sports as you have time for around the other demands on your time. It is relatively easy to learn such things when other teenagers are also. You find interesting future friends in each new activity in which you get involved, now and in later life. In order to make friends, you must go where they are and know what to do when you get there.

Popular people go out to others. Studies of what makes for popularity among teenagers find that it is the persons who are friendly who have the most friends. They smile at others and have a kind word even for casual acquaintances that make others glad to be near them. Shy or self-centered individuals do little to make others feel comfortable. They go their lonely way with downcast eyes that turn others off. Slow to offend and quick to forgive is a simple formula for success in building friendships. This may be one of the reasons why teenagers who remain active in church work tend more than others to have warm friends of both sexes . . . they have learned the secret of love in action.

Getting in Too Deep Too Fast

Teenagers and parents alike are concerned about not getting too involved too soon. Members of both generations realize that education should not be foreshortened by some ill-advised love affair. They look around them and see other young people caught in the traps of early marriage or emotional hangups, and they pray that such things not happen in their family.

Love-hungry teenagers are vulnerable. All young people need the loving attention of persons they care about. But, some teenagers are especially hungry for affection and do almost anything to get it. Children who have grown up in neglectful families long more than others for the tender loving care other children have known through the years. Teenagers who feel that their parents do not really care about them are apt to go overboard in their search for the deep personal caring they so desperately need.

Alvin's parents periodically separated several years before he became a teenager. They did not divorce, but continued to bicker with one another often in Alvin's hearing. In fact, his father and mother used him as a weapon in their threats of one another. This made Alvin feel that no one really cared anything about him as a person. He had borne so much of his parents' pain that he longed for the comfort of a caring relationship. This he found in Rosalee who sympathized with him as only a girl from a broken home could. They shared their mutual hurt and clung to one another with an intensity that was frightening. Alvin emerged from his affair with Rosalee full of compassion for her and with a wiser view of himself. He began to see that his parents' problem was not his to solve and that he must build his life more solidly than either his parents or he and Rosalee had. Fortunately he had the counsel of a wise minister who led him to more mature and truly loving paths into manhood.

Safeguarded situations when boy and girl friends meet are more important than most teenagers recognize. A girl sees nothing wrong in inviting her boyfriend into her home when he accompanies her home from school. They may be simply going to do their homework together, a perfectly innocent activity. But if there is no one else at home just then, the couple of kids place themselves in a highly vulnerable situation, regardless of how highly principled they are. Studies of situations in which teenagers become emotionally aroused and sexually active show that the girl's home is most frequently the site of their involvement.

What can a girl do if she knows that no one else is home? She can simply say, "I'd like to invite you in but it will have to be some other time." If the boy is considerate, he will not insist nor will he invite his girl friend to his home when no one else is there. He, too, has a great deal at stake in not getting in too deep, too fast. Many a teenager resents such simple safeguards, but experience indicates without question that they are worth taking.

Keeping one's cool while learning to love and be loved is a real art. Teenagers feel warmly about one another more often than not. They must learn how to keep their heads even when their hearts are throbbing with new emotions more powerful than any they have known before. They have to know how to put up a brave front even when they ache with loneliness inside. They have a great deal to learn about the attraction innately present between men and women, so that they can cope with it effectively when it becomes manifest. In any emotional upheaval, at least one of the parties involved must remain calm enough to act responsibly for both of them, if necessary. This often is the girl who has been taught to be restrained in expressing herself. It sometimes is the boy who realizes how much is at stake in throwing himself and his reputation away in some unworthy episode. Spiritual strength gives the sense of direction most young people need in the midst of temptation.

Problem Friendships

Teenagers, like persons of all ages, find themselves with ill-chosen friends and associates at one time or another. They come to sense that they have gotten into a bad situation. They say openly, "We are not good for one another." The reasons why a given friendship does not work out well may be many. It often can be seen for what it is as soon as the individuals involved are ready to look at it with clear heads.

Bad reputations are catching, unless redemption is part of the picture. Run around with one or more individuals who have been in serious trouble, and one risks sharing their reputation. The boy who joins a gang known as troublemakers is soon suspect. The girl who goes with a fellow who is a recognized user of drugs begins to be recognized as a drug-user too, even though she is innocent. The teenagers who get into a drinking crowd are generally seen as imbibing as well. This may not seem fair, but it is one of the facts of life that persons of all ages must understand. This is why parents are so adamant about their sons and daughters associating with young people whose reputations are unsullied.

There is a difference in earning a bad reputation oneself and having it thrust upon one by one's family or associates. Clarence came from a seamy side of town. His father hung around the local tavern; his mother entertained other men in ways that were considered quite indecent. Clarence made a real effort to shake off his unfavorable background but had a hard time of it because it clung to him wherever he went. It took Martha and her church group to give Clarence the chance he needed to create a more favorable image. It was not easy—for Clarence, for Martha, or for the young people's group at church. Many of the good church families looked askance at the participation of a young man from such a poor background. Fortunately, Martha's parents backed her in her faith in Clarence. The youth minister of the church befriended the boy and lived to see him ordained as a preacher of the gospel himself in time.

Friends of another faith, race, or nationality are still seen as potential problems. Let a girl be attracted to a boy from a quite different religious orientation, and she finds her family, his relatives, and her friends discouraging her seeing him. A teenager who gets involved with a person of a different race finds it hard to have him or her fully accepted by his family, his friends, or even his church. Most parents know that a couple from different races have more problems than those of the same color. Adults fear the possibility of interracial marriage in any friendship between a boy and a girl of different racial stock. They may be broadminded in accepting all persons as children of God and yet prefer that their own teenagers avoid the hazards of intimacy with members of a markedly different racial group.

Building a marriage or a friendship across wide gulfs of racial, religious, or ethnic difference is more difficult than establishing a lasting relationship with a person from a background like one's own. The wider the social distance between the two persons, the more adjustments they must make to meet one another on common ground. It can be done, of course. It is possible to love, enjoy, and live with a person who is quite unlike oneself in highly visible ways. It takes a deep core of similar interests and values to make such a pair feel close when their obvious characteristics are so dissimilar.

What attracts to an "impossible person"? This is a key question a teenager in an unpromising friendship of whatever kind should try to answer. What is it in me that responds to this individual so unlike others I have known? Is it the very difference that I find exciting? challenging? fulfilling? Is this a way in which I am rebelling from my parents and their teachings? Am I a better person for having such a friend? Or, am I somehow reduced in stature and insecure within myself in my association with this unlikely person?

Parents, already upset by the problem friendship, may not be as helpful to a teenager trying to discover its meaning as is a more objective counselor. A young person who really wants to discover his own motivation for establishing a relationship that is causing more pain than pleasure talks over his dilemma with a counselor at church, school, or guidance service. There he can work through what it is that the relationship means to him/her and then go on to deciding what to do about it.

Getting out of a problem friendship may worry a teenager. It is not a simple process. A young person does not want to hurt the other individual. Few teenagers like to feel shabby in shaking off another who may have been too close. The other person may cling and make it difficult to end the relationship. One may feel torn between a sense of loyalty and a feeling of what must be done. Whatever one does to terminate an unpromising friendship, it must be effective. It should be honest and sincere. It is best done quickly without undue agonizing about what might have been. If possible it should be the result of mutual discussion and agreement in ways that leave both of the pair stronger and better persons than they had been before.

Family Acceptance of Teen Friends

Fortunate is the teenager whose family welcomes his friends. He freely invites them home knowing that his family accepts them without question. There is no need to deceive his parents about who it is that he or she is seeing, for they welcome any friends of their children's.

Getting acquainted without prying is an art. Most parents want to know their children's friends and associates. They like to know about their family, their interests, their character. In their eagerness to get acquainted with the new friend brought into the teenager's home for the first time, the parents may ask too many questions. There is a fine line between showing interest and intruding into the other person's privacy. Wise parents are courteous in expressing interest in their children's guests, without offending them with too searching questions. Some of these background queries may be satisfactorily answered by their own teenager when first he or she speaks of the new friend about to be introduced to the family. Some will emerge in time without direct questioning. Some can be seen in the young friend's conduct and behavior. Much as adults respect one another in the process of getting acquainted, they are careful not to pry into their teenagers' associates overly much. Teenagers sometimes are unnecessarily touchy about a show of interest on the part of their parents in their friends. They must know that their family is interested and has a right to know whom their son or daughter is seeing.

Reasonable limits on family hospitality should be set. Parents like to have their teenagers' friends in the home. They prefer that their sons and daughters bring their friends home rather than meet them outside all the time. But there are limits to a family's patience and hospitality. Too many hungry teenagers can eat a family out of house and home. Thoughtless teenagers can ruin furnishings and wreck havoc in the household. Parents are wise to work out policies of entertaining with their teenagers whereby it is understood what may be consumed, and what is out of bounds. Some families have a snack shelf in the refrigerator that may be tapped for refreshments without infringing on what has been planned for the family's meals. Families have some informal area where teenagers can be entertained without doing costly damage to carpeting and furniture. Such things should be clearly understood by the family's teenagers.

Rules for the use of the family telephone have to be clear-cut and mutually agreed. It goes without saying that no visitor may monopolize the phone, make long-distance calls, or have calls transferred there without specific clearance with the parents ahead of time. So too, it is wise to have an agreement on the times when friends' calls are welcomed and when they are to be discouraged. If mealtime is important in a family, the parents and teenagers may establish a policy by which telephone calls are not taken when a meal is being served. Should a friend call at mealtime, he or she can simply be told: "We are at dinner now. May I call you back later?" When all family members observe such a ruling, it soon becomes an established practice that is relatively easy to enforce.

Including teenagers' friends in family outings works well in some families. The Johnsons have two teenagers—a boy and a girl. While the children were still little they were each allowed to invite a best friend along on a family picnic, trip to the zoo, or other family holiday. Now that the young people have almost grown up, the established practice is even more satisfying. The teenagers each have a favorite friend as companion on the outing. The parents get some peace and quiet of their own, with less fussing between the siblings, and better manners on the part of all the teenagers.

Teenagers enlarge the family circle when their families let them. There is nothing quite like the chatting and banter of good friends to reassure parents that all is well with their young people. When something disturbing does come up, it can be dealt with at once and with candor because of the uninterrupted communication that flows between the generations as well as within each of the age groups. Teenagers' friends bring something of the rest of the community with them when they are welcome in a home. Their parents represent other occupational, social, and community interests in some respects. Their language, conduct, and aspirations stretch a family's experience in the youth culture. Their perplexities and anxieties confirm parents' realization that such things are a normal part of the teen years. Their dreams and hopes and values give a lift to those of the family's own teenagers. The teen years are no time for a family to close its doors to others. Only as teenagers' best friends and sweethearts are welcome at home can the young people grow without restraint and go without leaving home in rebellion.

9
Sexual Episodes

Few areas of life are so confusing both to teenagers and to their parents as is sexual maturing. To teenagers it is a whole new door of life that is opening to them. They have been aware of themselves as members of one sex or the other all through their childhood. But with the coming of adolescence they develop into men and women with all the force, feelings, and fantasies of mature sexuality.

Sexuality in the Teens

Religious people believe that sexuality is a gift of God and a part of his creation. From their earliest exposure to the Bible they have heard and read the story of creation climaxed by the moving sentence: "So God created man in his own image, in the image of God he created him; male and female he created them" (Gen. 1:27, RSV). This being so, they have faith that sex in innately good and a central fact of life.

Sex is central in living and loving. Most young people grow up in families with members of both sexes of all ages in intimate interaction. They see Mother and Father living together, bearing and rearing their children, and facing life's stresses with courage because they love one another. They dream of someday becoming parents themselves and begin to think of members of the other sex as possible mates long before they are old enough to marry. They know love not only from their parents but also in many varied ways outside the family. They feel strongly attracted to special persons with an urgency that is both frightening and exciting. Before they are far into their teen years, they are deeply moved by strong love feelings they have never known before.

Romeo's Juliet was barely in her teens when she knew the tragedy of young love. Her feelings are mirrored in many another young teenager now. The dynamic force of such powerful love feelings is the maturing sex drive with which adolescents have not had previous experience. The elemental sexual urge manifests itself in maturing youth no matter what is done about it. It is there, just beneath the surface of their lives, whether they court it or not. It cannot be denied as an ever-present reality that surfaces at unexpected times, places, and contacts.

Sexual overtones emerge out of closeness to another person. Two teenagers can be busy studying when a casual touch of hand, foot, or knee can set off a torment of desire in the boy and a shiver of response in the girl. The contact may or may not have been deliberate. It does not even require actual touching. Ears, eyes, and nose sense the presence of a potential lover, and the flame is kindled. This short fuse of teenage sexual desire is not well enough understood by many teenagers. So, they are often dismayed and distracted when it occurs. Nice, well-brought up kids can feel guilty over the perfectly natural impulses they experience, until they have learned to recognize and deal with them in responsible ways.

Sexual urges can be kept within bounds. Most grown men and women have learned to recognize their sexual feelings and to express or to control them as they wish. Teenagers still have to learn how to identify the various sensations of their budding sexuality enough to keep them within the limits that are appropriate to the situation, the other individual, and their sense of who they are as persons.

Fortunate is the teenager who knows enough about himself to sense what is right for him. Happy is the girl who is sure enough of who she is to keep a clear head in the face of temptation. Wise are the parents who have helped their children find out what it means to be man or a woman and how members of the two sexes feel about one another and still be objective about their sex and love feelings. Once they are caught up in a torrent of passionate romance, it is too late to tell them very much. Adults can then only sit by and hope that their teenager's innate good sense will keep him or her from going overboard.

What Parents Fear

Parents naturally are protective of their teenagers. They love and care about them. They have nursed them through infancy and childhood. They want them to go through their teens without being seriously hurt. They see around them the disasters that older boys and girls have made of their lives, and they want to protect their sons and daughters from the tragedies of life if they can. They sense that their teenagers are caught up in strong emotions that are new to them. They realize that they cannot deny the presence of these powerful feelings. Nor can they turn them off by preaching or with too rigid restrictions. Their best hope is in facing their own fears and making themselves and their experience available to their teenagers in a spirit of loving candor.

Fear that they are losing their children is unconsciously a part of parents' anxiety. With the coming of adolescence, mothers regret seeing the end of childhood with its sweet dependence upon her and her husband as parents. Fathers sometimes admit regretting that their beloved daughters turn in their teens to other males for affection. Once Father was his little girl's first sweetheart, and now he has been replaced. He usually feels that the boy who so attracts his teenage daughter is not good enough for her. He often is downright critical of this usurper of his daughter's loving attention.

Teenagers must be patient with this highly understandable attitude on the part of one or both of their parents. They can see their parents' criticism of any young sweetheart they have as a reflection of their family's love. They can take their parents' anxiety as evidence of their devotion, and as a sincere compliment, even when it seems otherwise. It is not that parents distrust their teenagers, it is that they acknowledge the power of forces of which young people are not yet fully aware.

Anxiety about growing old is behind some parents' fears. They see their teenagers bright, young, attractive, and by comparison they may feel middle-aged, dull, and past their prime. They may resent the energy that youth throws away on "having fun," when they could use so well such vitality themselves. They feel old and tired before their time in the face of the bubbling enthusiasm of their teenagers. They would like to hold on to youth for a bit longer, but they can't. So they take out their frustration in fears of and for their teenagers.

A *fear of real dangers* in overt teenage sex is everpresent. Loving parents would like to keep their children from being hurt in their sexual development. They want to warn them of some of the real hazards to be avoided in sexual expression. They need not be excessive in their warnings. But modern parents sense that they must give their teenagers clear reasons for being cautious. Parents and teenagers alike benefit from talking out what it is they fear in adolescent sexual encounters. Only then can they become explicit enough to communicate with one another. By discussing what they are afraid of, some of the fear drains off, and they can relax in the comfort of knowing they have done what they could.

Pregnant Teenagers

Close to the surface in parental concern for their teenagers is their fear of teenage pregnancy. There is a solid basis for their concern. A good many girls become pregnant before they get married. There are more now than formerly by far, and they are younger, too. A social case worker with an agency for unmarried mothers in a large city says that when she began working there two decades ago most of the unmarried mothers were in their late teens or early twenties. Now it is not at all unusual to find girls coming in for help at age thirteen or even younger.

Teenage motherhood is a problem for the girl, her family, her boyfriend, and her baby. The pregnant school girl finds herself faced with the responsibility of caring for a baby or doing away with it, either of which is awesome in its prospects. Her education is curtailed, cut short, or terminated, even in communities making special provisions for pregnant school girls. She loses her status as a virgin and is thereafter known among exploitive males as a girl who does not say no. She is confronted with her changed image of herself, who she is, and what she wants to become.

A daughter's premarital pregnancy plunges her family into a complexity of difficult decisions. Will they insist that she marry the boy? Have they reason to believe this would be a good marriage? Should they urge her to have her baby and let them adopt it or place it for adoption? Are they willing and able to take on the responsibility of caring for an infant with all this entails? Could they go along with her decision to interrupt her pregnancy, with all the dangers inherent in an abortion, emotionally as well as physically? How can they help her restore faith in herself? In her ability to love and to be loved? In her rebuilding of confidence in life itself?

The boy in the case has his problems, too. He is often but a shadowy figure in the background of the girl's dilemma. He may be in fact if he slips out of the picture as soon as he learns that she is pregnant. But, if he cares about the girl, he regrets the predicament in which he has placed her. He feels like a heel and wants to make amends if he can. So, he tells her he is willing to marry her to give the baby a name and to protect her. This may be the last thing he really wants to do. He might have to cut short his education and get a job to support his young family or take his parent's reluctant help in order to finish school. He may be afraid of the responsibilities becoming a father involves when he has not found himself fully as yet.

Marriage forced by the girl's pregnancy is risky. Teenage

marriages generally are less successful than marriage of more mature young people. The have-to marriage is the most vulnerable of all. Each may blame the other for their condition. Recriminations and guilty denials are hurtful both before and after marriage. Both of the pair may be, indeed usually are, quite unready to take on the triple tasks of building a marriage, establishing a family, and launching themselves into their life work while they are still teenagers. Their families are rarely happy about their plight, and sometimes disown them completely, or parents may make life so miserable for the young parents that they almost wish they were entirely on their own. With so much against teenage pregnancy, the next pertinent question is how it can be avoided.

Preventing Teenage Pregnancies

[This section is not intended to encourage premarital or extramarital sexual intercourse. Rather, it is written to help parents, and teenagers, have a better understanding of means of preventing pregnancies.]

The best way to avoid pregnancy is to abstain from sexual intercourse. This is a clear statement of fact upon which all authorities agree. The more sexual intimacy, the greater the possibility of pregnancy. A girl may have one or two sexual experiences without losing more than her virginity. But if she continues to be initimate with one boy, or several, the chances are she will become pregnant in time; unless she is competent in avoiding pregnancy by responsible use of an effective contraceptive.

Girls' use of contraceptives is notoriously inadequate. Many teenagers prefer to feel "it won't happen to us." They would rather risk pregnancy than to cold-bloodedly do anything to prevent it. If sexual intercourse does occur, the couple like to believe that "it just happened." If they protect themselves beforehand, it somehow seems not quite nice.

There are few contraceptives that are completely fool-proof and safe for a teenage girl. She finds a diaphragm, foams, jellies, and other traditional female protections messy, hard to use at the time, and requiring privacy she often does not have at home or the site of her rendezvous. The intrauterine device (IUD) is rarely available to her. Nor is it easy for a girl to get a prescription for the contraceptive pill. This takes the combined cooperation of her mother, her physician, and herself, any of whom may resist taking the step. Using the pill effectively means taking it each and every day for the prescribed number of days each month—or she might as well not take it at all. There is a price to pay beyond the cost of the pills themselves. Some girls and women put on weight and undergo other unpleasant side effects when they are on the pill. The girl known to be taking the pill is subject to unwelcome advances from exploitative males of all ages—advances that make her feel cheap. It may be better than getting pregnant, but there must be a better way.

Male contraceptives are no more effective than are those the girl uses. The condom, or "rubber" as it is popularly known, can slip off, be punctured, or be applied too late to catch the sperm that precede the main ejaculation. It lessens the fellow's satisfaction, and he finds it a nuisance to apply at the time of his erection. Coitus interruptus, in which the penis is withdrawn from the vagina before ejaculation, is not satisfactory, and requires discipline beyond the ability of most teenage boys. In spite of all the discussion, there is no male pill that renders a boy infertile. Nor is there a "morning after" pill to be recommended at this writing. When one is available, it doubtless will require a prescription, limiting its use to married couples or victims of rape and other special cases.

"The safe period" cannot be relied upon completely. The rhythm method is based upon the regularity of the female's cycle of menstruation and ovulation. Normally a girl menstruates every twenty-eight days or so. Midway between her menstruals when she ovulates she is most likely to become pregnant. Theoretically the rhythm method works, because if there is no ovum in her genital tract, she cannot get pregnant that

month. The trouble is that a girl's menstrual cycle is not always regular. Often it is quite unreliable. A cold, an emotional upset, a crisis in her family or in her own life can either delay or bring on her period in ways that cannot be counted upon. Even married women whose cycles are more regular than teenagers find that "the safe period" is not safe enough for them to rely on if they must avoid pregnancy.

Parents have strong feelings about preventing the pregnancy of their daughters. Some mothers insist that their girls be fitted with a diaphragm, or be given a supply of pills, or an IUD before they go off to summer camp where they might be exposed to temptation. Other parents rely on their daughter's good judgment, and prefer to trust her than to so obviously question her future conduct. Most parents hope that their sons and daughters will go through the teen years without getting into trouble, sexually or otherwise. They know that pregnancy is but one of the results of sexual activity, and do what they can to protect their teenagers from being damaged by overt sex expression.

Rape—Reality and Safeguards

Rape is the crime no one wants to talk about. Until recently it was rarely discussed above a whisper. But now so many girls and women are sexually assaulted, it can no longer be ignored. Rape is a serious, frightening, and violent crime against girls and women. Its victims find the experience debasing, painful, and emotionally distressing. Females of all ages have been victims of rape. Although it is not solely a teenage hazard, girls should know how to protect themselves from this critical danger.

Avoiding break-ins at home is part of a family's safety precautions. Children and teenagers should be taught to require identification of all repairmen and utility workers before admitting them. Members of the family should keep the doors locked and the drapes pulled when they are home alone. Mysterious or obscene telephone calls should be reported to the local law enforcement agency. It is not wise to tell a telephone caller or someone at the door that there is no one else at home. When caring for children in another family's home, it is best not to allow anyone else in the house while the owners are away. It is better to be safe than sorry, especially in situations where the hazards are so great.

Safety on the street can be taught girls by their mothers even before they reach the teen years. Girls should know enough not to go into poorly lit streets, alleys, vacant lots, or buildings that are not occupied. A girl's best defense is having other people nearby. She should be warned against accepting rides from strangers and from hitchhiking. It is cheaper to take a taxi or call her family to send for her than it is to risk all that might happen in a stranger's automobile. Two or more girls traveling together are safer than one alone, but they too should follow precautions for their safety.

Possible attacks in an automobile should be prevented by teenagers who drive. It is best to have your car key in hand before leaving the building. Next, check the floor of the back seat for intruders before getting into the automobile. Keep car doors locked and windows up when driving. If your car is being followed, drive to a busy well-lit business establishment and call the police. If you have car trouble, signal for help by raising the car hood, and remain inside with doors locked until identified help arrives. Should another motorist offer help, roll down the window an inch and ask him to call the police or sheriff's department. Make sure there is enough gas in the car at all times, so that no one in the family will risk running out of fuel in some potentially dangerous place.

Getting away from an attacker is a possibility for a girl who does not panic. She may be able to talk her way out of being molested, while she looks for a way to escape. Then it is best to scream "FIRE!" which more people react to immediately than to anything else. It is not recommended that a teenage girl or young women physically resist her attacker unless she knows how to immobilize him at once. A knee to his groin, a sharp blow to his nose, or his finger bent back until he releases her may give her the chance she needs to run away. Many girls and women today learn even more sophisticated methods of resisting attack in self-defense programs in schools, youth groups, and community agencies.

Reporting a rapist's attack is not easy for a girl or her family. They dread the notoriety and hate to get involved. Yet by this time they *are* involved and should do what they can to protect other girls and women from being similarly assaulted. Therefore, it is best to immediately report any rape or attempted rape to prevent this man from victimizing other girls in the future. While waiting for the police a girl should not change her clothes, wash, or apply medication. The physical evidence will be important in the prosecution. Full cooperation with the police in the investigation and trial is necessary, since the victim's testimony is essential to conviction. Remember rape is a crime of hate, never of love. It is dehumanizing, humiliating, and may lead to murder.

Teaching boys to respect girls is one recommendation of the executive director of the National Organization for the Prevention of Rape. He finds that 35 percent of the girls and women attacked are victims of their own boyfriends, fiances, or dates. Another 35 percent are raped by someone they know in some other way: the father's boss or subordinate, a teacher, neighbor, or friend of the family. He advocates bringing up boys to treat every date as if it were her last night on earth and give her a beautiful time. Girls should neither be unduly suspicious nor seductive in their encounters with boys and men. As members of both sexes learn to respect themselves and one another, crimes against others might be reduced.

VD Among Teenagers

Venereal disease is an epidemic of vast proportions. Every three minutes twenty-three young people aged fifteen through nineteen became infected with gonorrhea, in a recent year. Young people under twenty-five account for nearly half of the thousands of new cases of syphilis reported each year. Gonorrhea and syphilis are by far the most damaging diseases passed on through sexual activity. But even more common sexually transmitted complaints are inflammation of the urethra or vagina, pubic lice called "crabs," and herpes genitalia which can be acutely painful.

Nice kids get VD. No longer can Americans hide behind the myth that only prostitutes and their customers get infected. Today, venereal disease is so prevalent that almost any teenager having sexual intercourse with first date or favorite companion can become infected. Sons and daughters of good families are under great pressure today to become sexually experienced. Members of both sexes are told by their peers that everyone is doing it and that not to go all the way is to be a prude or worse. The mood is one in which it is hard for a teenager who wants to wait for love and marriage to hold to his or her standards. Sexual activity is widely advertised along with toothpaste and toiletries for members of both sexes. Popular music, movies, and magazines assume that sex is for everyone, anytime, with no holds barred. Supervision of mixed pairs and social groups is not as tight as once it was. So, many nice youngsters from good families find, to their dismay, that they have lost their virginity and picked up a dose of VD.

Venereal disease can be cured if it is treated in time. The sad fact is that all too often a teenager is ashamed to report the sexual act that might have resulted in infection. He or she ignores the annoying first symptoms of gonorrhea (burning sensation when urinating, vaginal discharge, or signs so unclear that girls often are not aware of what is happening) until the disease advances into the genital tract where it can cause serious damage. Left untreated gonorrhea can cause sterility, peritonitis, and the pain of arthritis.

The first evidence of syphilitic infection appears two or more weeks after the sexual activity in the form of a painless chancre at the site of the contact. Later a secondary stage sets in with a rash, sores in the mouth, headache, fever, sore throat, or all of these together. This stage may pass with little discomfort, but the spirochetes do not go away. They remain in the body for years to emerge as blindness, insanity, heart disease, or paralysis in the person decades after he or she has become infected.

Modern treatment for venereal infection is simple, painless, and effective if the individual goes early for examination and treatment. A teenager is wise to go to the local health clinic or to his or her own physician after having had sexual intercourse. Competent medical attention is essential for effective treatment. There is nothing that can be bought at the drug store that will cure either gonorrhea or syphilis. The examining doctor will not only treat the patient but is expected to find out with whom the infected person has had intercourse so that they too may be treated. Only in that way can the diseases be kept from going like wildfire through the teenage population.

Preventing venereal infection is much like avoiding pregnancy. Abstinence is the only sure way of avoiding venereal disease or pregnancy. The next most reliable way is being sure that one's sexual partner is not infected. It is not possible to tell whether the other person is disease-free by looking at him or her, by relying on his good reputation alone, or by anything except trust in the reliability and loyalty of the other person. Married couples who have remained faithful to one another before and after marriage have no fear of contracting VD. All others could possibly be a source of infection, whether or not they are aware of it.

For those who take chances, the use of condom by the male and germicidal vaginal creams, jellies, and foam by the female reduce the risk of catching a disease through sexual contact. None of these is perfect, and any may fail to give the needed protection. Washing carefully after exposure may help, but it is ineffective as a preventive in most cases. The only sure way to avoid VD is to avoid sexual activity with persons and in situations where risk is present. It helps to know enough about sexual health and disease to live without unnecessary fears, secure in one's understanding of oneself and in one's understanding of other persons.

Education in Life and Love

The best education for living and loving is in the home, augmented by programs in church, school, and community groups. Children and teenagers who have been reared in families where the parents obviously love one another, and where all family members are accepted for themselves have a built-in background of security. They are not so likely to take to extremes as are youngsters from less stable homes. They find it easier to acquire the knowledge, develop the skills, attitudes, and values that give them a positive approach to life and its problems.

Knowledge about the sex side of life is surprisingly difficult for teenagers to acquire. They have grown up in a culture filled with distorted sexual allusions in press, films, television, and conversation. They have been exposed to confusing realities of the sex side of life long before they became old enough to understand them fully. Their friends have told them much that is not so. They feel under pressure to act sophisticated, yet all too often quake with uncertainty within. Many teenagers are reticent about asking questions or discussing their confusions with parents or other responsible adults. Some parents are reluctant to talk freely with their children about life and love. So ignorance and half-truths abound in the teenage generation.

Ignorance is not bliss, especially in vital areas of living, loving, and relating to others in meaningful ways. That is why many churches hold group sessions for their children and teenagers in which areas of personal intimacy and moral issues may be discussed. Schools have come a long way in classes for boys and girls on what it means to grow up and how members of both sexes feel about their relationships at various levels. YMCA's and other community agencies hold programs for fathers and sons, for mothers and daughters, and for mixed groups of parents and teenagers on subjects of interest to members of both generations. These are often easier to discuss under competent leadership and a comfortable small group atmosphere than on a one-to-one basis between parent and teenager.

Personal and social skills are an asset. Teenagers find themselves in a wide variety of situations where knowing what to do and how to act saves them embarrassment. Both girls and boys need to know how to carry on a conversation, accept and refuse invitations gracefully, cope with jealousy, and deal with unwelcome behavior of a too eager companion in sexually exciting situations. Today's young people should know where life's hazards are, how to avoid them whenever possible, how to escape them, and what to do when they need help. This takes skill of a high order. Without minimal competence in these areas of potential harm to oneself and others, a teenager is vulnerable amidst dangers too great to risk.

Attitudes of caution and respect are powerful allies against harm. Teenagers who have learned to love and respect other persons with appropriate caution against hurting them or themselves neither freeze with fear nor dash into danger needlessly. They understand enough of the seamy side of life to prefer lives that are wholesome, productive, and happy. They absorb such attitudes from their parents without realizing it. Only those families whose attitudes turn off their teenagers lose their influence in instilling the basic attitudes toward life.

Values worth living for are central in a teenager's inner security. As he values himself, he does not throw himself or herself needlessly away in trivial hedonism. As he cares for other people of all ages and both sexes, he shows them the consideration they respond to with appreciation. As he cherishes the goodness of life, as she looks forward to life unfolding beyond and within her, teenagers of both sexes thrill to the miracle of living within their grasp. Such value systems accept the mystery of life and love with a sense of stewardship. The physical body is viewed as too precious to harm, and the spirit too sacred to tarnish. Religion does a great deal to promote such values, and is a family's ally in guiding its children through their teen years.

10
Money Matters Between Parents and Teens

"Money, money, money, that's all I hear from you these days, and already you cost us more than your two younger brothers put together!" This father's explosion might not have been wise, but it reflects realities in families with teenagers. It is generally true that family outlay for teenagers is more than that for younger children. Teenagers have insatiable appetites to feed their fast-growing bodies. Food costs for them exceed those of other family members. Clothing, transportation, and recreation costs zoom during the teen years, until a father may wonder how he can make ends meet, even before a teenager puts in a plea for more money to spend.

American teenagers spend billions of dollars annually to meet their personal needs. Boys spend most of their cash for clothing, cameras, and car costs. Girls put most of their available money into grooming aids and clothes. Both sexes have expenses for school supplies, records, snacks, school lunches, and entertainment. Teenagers' need for money increases throughout the teen years so that by nineteen a typical teenager is spending ten times as much as he or she did at age twelve, according to economists' calculations. No wonder money matters so much for members of both generations in the family.

Allowances—Pro and Con

Opinions about giving a teenager a regular allowance vary widely. Some parents prefer to give each of their children an allowance, and others will have none of it. Some teens like to know what they can count on and when, others think they get more by "putting the bite on" their parents for money as they need it. There are advantages and disadvantages in both systems.

An allowance is a definite amount of money given at regular intervals to meet personal needs. The teenager then has the responsibility of apportioning the amount available to him over the various items he or she must pay for. When a teenager has had an allowance all through the years that he or she has been growing up, he and his parents know what they can expect of one another. Usually the amount of the allowance increases as a child grows older and his costs are greater. During the teen years, consumption of goods and services is at its peak, and presumably the allowance is larger than ever. How much is dependent upon the family's affluence, what the teenager feels he needs, and the process of negotiation between parent and teenager.

What the allowance covers should be clearly understood by both parents and teenager. Minimally, a child's allowance covers his school costs and some spending money for which he does not have to account. As children become teenagers, their allowance may also cover their clothing needs in whole or in part. Other items included in some family allowance agreements are travel, car costs, contributions to various school and community drives for funds, and money for church. Usually not included are such expenses as medical and dental bills and other items considered part of the whole family budget.

When unexpected costs must be met by a teenager beyond those agreed upon for the allowance, special negotiations are in order. Tod was in a dilemma when his new all-weather jacket was stolen. He had carefully laid aside money for it from his allowance and had done comparison shopping for it in a way that pleased his parents. Then, before it was two weeks old it disappeared somewhere at school. When it did not turn up, it became obvious that it had to be replaced. Tod did not have enough money to buy another jacket so soon,

yet he needed one now. His parents made an arrangement
with him by which they forwarded him the money for a new
jacket which he repaid out of his allowance over the next
few weeks. This impressed upon Tod the importance of protecting personal property as much as possible, at the same
time that it helped him meet the unexpected cost of buying
another new jacket that month.

Teenagers are as financially responsible as they have learned
to be. When they have learned through the years to live within
a budget, they know what is involved in making an allowance
stretch over their anticipated expenses. Teenagers sometimes
run short before the next allowance is due and then must either
do without, ask for an advance, or float a loan from their
parents. If parents consistently bail out their teenagers from
their financial embarrassments, full maturity in monetary matters is delayed. Yet unnecessary deprivation cannot be ad-
vocated. The Wilkins thought they were teaching their son
character when they refused to give him an advance on his
allowance. Then they learned that he had gone without lunch
at school all·week and stayed home from church because he
did not have money for the plate. A family conference cleared
the matter, with each understanding the other better for it.

Allowance periods are adjusted to the ability of the particular
person's ability to plan expenditures over a length of time.
A little child's allowance may be for a few days or a week.
By the teen years, an allowance may be on a monthly basis
or even longer. The Lanes kept careful accounts of clothing
outlays for each member of the family over the years. When
their Vi felt she was ready for money to cover her next year's
clothing costs, she and her parents knew how much had been
spent annually for her clothes. That amount was increased
somewhat in recognition of higher prices, and Vi was given
a check to cover all her clothes for the coming year. Never
was a girl more careful of how she spent her money than
was Vi. She shopped for bargains and soon was making her
own blouses, skirts, and school clothes. She consulted her

mother and planned with her girl friends on the best buys for shoes, rain wear, and tailored outfits. By the time she went to college, she was a competent shopper and a clever seamstress, thanks to her family's willingness to let her take over her clothing budget when she felt she was ready.

Give Me Money When I Need It

Occasionally a teenager opts against having an allowance. He or she may not want the responsibility of planning the expenditures the allowance is supposed to cover. Parents may encourage their children to come to them for what they want, when they want it, so that the teenager has had little or no experience in handling his own money over a period of time.

Doling out what a teenager needs when he or she asks for it has the advantage of keeping the parents informed about what their teenager says money is needed for. It has the disadvantage of making the young person appeal for funds as needs arise and running the risk of being turned down when parents do not meet the request. Being refused frustrates a teenager and makes parents feel put upon when an angry scene eventuates. Another problem is the skill with which teenagers may pit one parent against the other in their request for money. One parent is often more openhanded than the other. Either may be in a better mood than the other on a particular occasion. One parent can accuse the other of indulging their teenager unduly. So, in many a family the dole system of giving teenagers their money results in scheming and other unhappy situations between family members.

Parents hold the purse strings in families where teenagers are given money as they request it. This has the advantage of keeping the decision in the hands of the parents who have earned the money. It has the disadvantage of keeping the teenagers dependent upon their parents for longer than otherwise might be necessary. It may make the young person especially persuasive in making his case, and at the same time pit teenager against parents in considering the appeal. It may or may not result in the youngster's getting more money in the long run than an allowance would have meant.

Paying Teenagers for Work at Home

Parents generally would like their teenagers to know the value of a dollar. They know what it means to work for what they have, and they want their children to share the experience of earning money when they are old enough to do so. When few jobs for teenagers are to be found in a community, the question arises should teenagers be paid for work they do around home?

Regular chores by family members are assumed by each person in the household without thought of payment. Such daily tasks as helping with meal preparation, clearing and doing the dishes, removing trash and taking out the garbage, making beds, and keeping rooms in order can be equitably divided among the various family members in terms of time available, interest, ability, and special considerations such as some rotation to keep boredom to a minimum. These are the things that are necessary to keep the family going, and therefore not to be negotiated for payment in most homes.

Paying jobs around the home can include any that a family might hire done. Such things as window washing, floor cleaning, car washing and waxing, yard work, painting, garage cleaning, and the like are such that in many families are contracted out. When there are teenagers in the home with need of cash and the time and competence to take on some of these paying jobs, they can be a source of income for the young people. Problems may arise when a given job takes up more time than a teenager should spare from his studies or when the work is poorly done. So, there is some sense in having a specific contract for a particular job that details what is to be done, when, and according to what standards.

Letting a family contract to one of its teenagers can be an experience in the business world for him and his family. At the time that the Prossers' garage needed painting, their son was keen on buying a guitar. Bids were received from local painters for the painting job, and Junior was asked if he, too, wanted to submit a bid. He jumped at the chance and put in the lowest bid for the paint, labor, ladder, and other equipment. He and his parents agreed upon the quality of paint, and the date by which the job should be completed. Junior made a work-study schedule that assured his parents he could paint the garage without sacrificing his homework and music lessons. It worked out well for both Junior and his parents. It brought in not only the money for the guitar but also a new sense of stature of the young man in the family.

Teenager's Earnings

Teenagers have other sources of money besides those received from their parents. Other relatives and family friends give them cash for Christmas, birthdays, and other special events. Many teenagers find ways of earning money in their spare time in the neighborhood. This not only opens up new sources of money, it also poses further questions for family discussion.

What teenagers do to earn money depends upon the community in which they live, their age, competence, and family standards. Baby-sitting is usually considered safe for both the young children and the teenager, as long as there is a clear understanding of what is expected. Many families request that the teenager staying with their children not entertain other young people in their home while they are away. This is important as a safeguard both for the teenager and for the younger children. Rates are discussed in advance, with special arrangements made for late hours and seeing the teenage girl safely home when the parents return. Classes in baby and child care are being offered in many communities for teenagers who want to upgrade their baby-sitting skills.

Teenagers of both sexes deliver morning and afternoon newspapers, work part-time in local stores, and sometimes are able to get full-time jobs through vacation periods. Such things are generally accepted as suitable for teenagers. Other jobs are more risky and, therefore, subject to parent-teen agreement.

Russ was offered a good paying job with a local tavern's combo. It called for his being there from five in the afternoon until midnight five nights a week. His parents objected to his taking the job because they felt it took time he needed for his school work, it would cut into his much needed rest, and it would expose him to a stratum of society that might be potentially dangerous. Russ was indignant at his parents' opposition and protested vigorously that he was old enough to take care of himself in such a situation. One week after the family fuss about it, the tavern was raided by the local authorities for illegal drug sales. This sobered Russ and was a lesson learned without harm, thanks to his parents' persistence in maintaining family standards of conduct.

Parents are legally responsible for their minor children. If anything happens to one of their teenagers, it is they who are blamed. Fortunately, most parents have the experience and the wisdom to guide their teenagers away from potentially dangerous situations. When they oppose something they feel unsuitable for their young people, there is usually some good reason for their objection. It is not that they do not trust their teenager but rather that they suspect that the situation is too risky just then.

Spending-saving balance for present and future needs is a part of the allocation of funds. There is a general feeling among adults that teenagers want to spend every cent they get as soon as they get it. This is an unfortunate generalization. Many teenagers are quite conservative in their spending and saving patterns. When thousands of teenagers were surveyed on the question, "If someone gave you $5,000, what would you do with it?" three fourths of them responded, "Put it in the bank." About 15 percent of the boys would spend some of the money for an automobile. Approximately 25 percent of the girls would give to church, charity, or family out of such a windfall.

Teenagers differ greatly in their spending-saving habits. Matt will not spend a dollar unless he has to. He is saving everything he can get his hands on for his future education. His cousin is just the opposite, spending money as though there were no tomorrow.

Funds for special purposes motivates many a teenager to save. It is easier to work toward a particular goal than just to save in the abstract. A teenager saving for something special he wants will do jobs to earn money he or she would not think of tackling without the incentive. Once in hand, these earnings go automatically into the special fund without intense competition of present pleasure. A family can encourage saving for special projects by adding something to a teenager's fund from time to time, by expressing their approval, and by serving as models in saving not only for a rainy day, but also for the bright things in life.

Meeting Automobile Costs

A car is apt to be terribly important to a teenage boy. With it he can feel free and independent. He can invite a girl out without having to rely on other transportation or a search for privacy through an evening. Many a lad likes a car for its own sake—for the feeling of power under the hood, the exhilaration of speed on the highway, the freedom to go and come as he likes, and the satisfaction of a smooth running engine. A teenager spends many a grimy hour tuning up his motor, adjusting a carburetor, or replacing a worn part with something he found in a junked automobile. Such discipline builds character as well as a vehicle, as many a father knows from firsthand experience.

Should a teenager have his own car? This question haunts a family as soon as a boy begins to yearn for a car of his own. He may still ride his bike around the neighborhood, but if he goes "where the action is," he needs a car. This means using the family automobile with all that is involved in sharing it responsibly with others in the family who drive. Or, it means having a car of his own to drive. Some affluent families give their sons or daughters their own automobiles as soon as they are old enough to have a license. Such a course is expensive, not only for the original cost of the car but also especially for its upkeep. Gas, oil, repairs, and insurance mount up beyond many a family's ability to meet the costs of the teenage driver. Accidents and dangers on the road for which many teenagers are not prepared give parents pause, even when they might afford the financial burden.

Parents foresee some of the problems owning a car might pose for their son. He might spend so much time in and on his car that his studies would suffer. Studies show clearly that there is justification for this parental anxiety. Teenagers generally tend to let their school work slide as soon as they have their own car. It takes an especially responsible teenager to avoid the temptation to go off for a drive when he should be studying for a test. Parents worry that their teenager might drive recklessly, thereby endangering himself and others. Fathers and mothers tend to be concerned not only about what might happen when their teenager's car is in motion; they worry quite as much when their teenager parks.

A *car offers teenagers privacy* beyond that afforded by the front porch or the back parlor couples resorted to in earlier times. A few minutes away from the garage in today's community, and teenagers are on their own. Where they go, what they do, and with whom is no longer supervised by the adults who know and care about them. They are subject to the risks their most adventurous friends suggest with few restraints upon them. Wherever they go, they may be confronted with situations calling for mature judgment and control. Drive-in movies, so popular with the younger generation, are known as "passion pits" for obvious reasons. Musical "happenings" are marked not only by the beat of the times but also the drugs that turn on the performers and audience alike. Now when chaperones and adult supervisors have given way to monitoring by police or sheriff's office, groups of teenagers or a couple in a car can be picked up for questioning at any time.

Carl and Beth were stopped one evening as they left their hometown on the way to camp to pick up Beth's younger brother. The patrolman signaled them over to the side of the road with his red lights flashing. Carl was scared, because he remembered the six-pack in the back seat. Sure enough, the cop spotted it, gave Carl a breath-o-lator test, questioned both of the pair, and then phoned the camp to verify their story. It was embarrassing for both the young people and their families. They could see that the cop was only doing his duty, but it was humiliating nevertheless. Had the six-pack been a few reefers, the young couple could have been in for even more than questioning in many a town.

Responsibility for the use of the family car is a familiar way of giving experience in what it entails. Parents have a right to expect that their automobile will be returned home in good shape after a teenager's use of it. When an accident occurs the teenager must remain at the scene until released by the authorities. Even when the damage is slight, it should be reported immediately to the car's owner and arrangements made for suitable repairs. Keeping the gas level up is important, especially when two or more family members have the use of the automobile. It is exasperating for a busy father to find himself out of gas on a busy thoroughfare when he is on the way to an important meeting. Teenagers who used the car the evening before are wise to stop for gas before returning home, thereby protecting the father and themselves from an unpleasant scene.

Families who share the family car with their teenage sons and daughters tend to expect help in keeping the automobile presentable. Teens who regularly wash and polish the car without prodding find their parents far more willing to let them have the keys when they need them than do those who abuse the privilege.

Insurance rates are higher when a teenager drives a family vehicle. The reason is found in comparative accident rates of hundreds of thousands of drivers of all ages. Nationally, young men under twenty-five have more accidents than do more mature men. So insurance companies have to charge more when a teenager has the use of a car. The family's question then is who pays the added amount for automobile insurance? The teenager who now uses the car upon occasion? His parents? Or both of them together according to a formula that is jointly discussed and agreed?

Kip works every year to pay his share of the insurance and other costs incident to his sharing the use of the family car. When he needs it for some special function, he clears with his parents ahead of time so that they will not be inconvenienced. They pay the same amount of insurance they were charged before Kip started to drive, with Kip putting in the remainder. They try to be reasonable in sharing the car when Kip needs it, without letting him take it over completely. They remember the definition of a pedestrian as a man with one car and two teenagers and protect their own interests as well as his.

Parental controls for teenagers' driving make sense. No family wants its car smashed up or its teenager badly injured. Most parents, therefore, institute minimal controls on their teenager's driving. For example: putting studies first as a primary responsibility of the teen years; delaying extensive driving privileges until the late teens; making sure that their teenager takes a defensive driving course and has a valid drivers' license before he or she has the use of the family's car or a car of his own; sharing the family car with mutually agreed limitations and controls; helping each teenager feel a sense of worth as a person so he will not have to "prove himself" behind the wheel of a fast-moving automobile.

Costs of College and Further Training

College-bound teenagers tend to be future-oriented in their management of money. Because college means much to them, they can forego immediate satisfactions for the greater benefits that lie ahead. Sons and daughters of college graduates tend to expect that they too will go to college, often to the alma mater of one of their parents. Families who are ambitious for their children dream of college for them long before they are old enough to go. Other families question the value of college for young people in general or for a given teenager in particular. Similarly, some young people are eager to go to college while others resist being pressured into it. So the question of training after high school is one that requires consideration of many factors for an individual teenager. One of the most pressing aspects is, "Can we afford it?"

College costs are spiraling all across the country. It is easier to get into college than it used to be, but bills run a lot higher. So parents and teenagers in many a family weigh the possibilities carefully before registration day.

Work-study plans are offered by many colleges and universities in the United States. The Federal government has allocated millions of dollars for such cooperative education programs in recent years. The plans differ, but essentially they provide the student an opportunity to work off campus several months a year while doing the usual college work on campus the rest of the year. Students graduate in five years more or less with less strain on the family budget and the advantage of having had experience in the work-a-day world while earning a bachelor's degree.

Some students opt for two years in a local junior college where they can get their basic college-level work out of the way at lower cost than going away to live as freshmen. Public community colleges give many students a chance for college-level work without too great a financial strain. Surveys show that community college graduates do well in senior college, graduate, and professional training if they have the ability and motivation to continue their education beyond high school.

Alternatives to college are being considered by many teenagers today. There are teenagers with few academic interests who prefer to get out of high school and into something that matters more to them. There are opportunities in some communities for young people interested in getting into auto mechanics, television repair, and similar apprentice-like experiences. Others, young men and women, too, sign up for military service out of high school, with the hope perhaps of going back to school later on.

Teenagers from families who can financially afford it in recent years have been taking a year off for travel before settling down into serious study for a future career. This option can be risky unless the young person is responsible enough to take advantage of the travel experience. News stories abound with reports of American teenagers congregating in European cities where they are unwashed, unfed, undisciplined, and unrelated to anything with meaning for them or others.

Still other teenagers find what work is available at minimum wages and take correspondence courses or guided self-study in their time off, until they find themselves ready to settle down to prepare for a career. Whatever the route a teenager takes, he or she is wise to discuss it and its alternatives with the family. More than he realizes at the moment, his future and theirs is bound together in most instances.

Heading in a direction is a general principle that guidance counselors recommend. Whether a teenager goes immediately into college upon finishing high school or delays for a year or so until he is ready, financially and otherwise, he is wise to choose a course that leads him toward his central interests and talents. Then the experience he or she gets in volunteer, military, or temporary work can be of value in testing a field of endeavor, and providing experience in it before total commitment is made.

Sol was not sure that he wanted to get into the long, expensive training that would be necessary for a degree in veterinary medicine when he finished high school. He got a job with a poultry farmer to try himself out in an actual farm situation. He found himself getting more and more excited about the future in veterinary research and practice, and after one year on the job, registered at a nearby state university. He was fortunate in getting a scholarship which with his savings from his job helps him make ends meet. His parents back his effort and are proud of having a son of theirs at the university—the first one of their family ever to go to college.

Family ambition and teenage preferences do not always mesh. Before parents become too set on their son going to college, it makes sense for them to explore with him what his own inclinations are. If he resists higher education in favor of something less abstract, that should be an important element to consider. Or take the opposite situation. There are parents who feel that education is wasted on a girl, because she'll get married anyway as soon as she graduates. Ruth, growing up in such a family, yearned for college and all it meant in getting up and away from home. She was ambitious for a professional career and fortunately was bright enough to have what it takes to succeed in it. Her pastor and his wife encouraged her in her struggle to go to college and proudly took her to the campus when her parents were "too busy." In time, her parents were proud of her progress, and her church kept closely in touch with her as one of their most devoted young people.

College and further preparation for life represents a major investment in time, money, and commitment. They are not to be entered into lightly but with as much consideration as is possible on the part of the teenager, the parents, and those other adults who are interested. Generalizations about what other families do or how other teenagers answer the questions for themselves are often not too relevant. What matters is who the teenager feels he or she is and what he wants to do about it.

11
Favoritism in the Family

Parents often are astounded to discover that one or more of their children feel less loved than the others. Yet this is a common situation. Teenaged Roy and Lucie are a case in point. Roy feels that his mother favors Lucie and puts him down with critical comparisons. Lucie, acknowledging her mother's favorable attention, feels that her father does not understand her and prefers her brother's company to hers.

Playing favorites over the years is familiar to many a family member. One child is especially favored by one of the parents and the other children sense it. Another youngster is chronically in the doghouse and knows it. Years later the same favoritism is apparent, accompanied by similar efforts on the part of the one less favored to gain equivalent attention from the parents. There is a tendency for boys in the family to model themselves after their father. This is all very well until Mother and Dad have a spat, when both father and son are apt to be criticized. Girls frequently pattern themselves after their mothers and become more and more like them as the years go by. This endears them to their fathers, in some instances. In others it operates in the opposite way with Father's displeasure with his wife affecting his feelings about his daughter as well. It is bad enough having to compete with one's brother or sister for a just share of one's parents' love without being unfavorably compared from time to time with a rival sibling.

Love and attention of parents for their children are not

142 luxuries that can be taken for granted. They are essential building blocks of personality. Every child needs to feel that his parents love him, as he is, for himself. Each child in the family struggles for parental recognition and warmth. If it comes easily, the youngster can relax, secure in the feeling that he belongs and is accepted. If a child or a teenager feels that his parents do not love him as much as they do other children in the family, he may bitterly resent the more favored child. This basic frustration is a cause of bickering between the children of the family. It is a basis of complaints that parents are not fair in dealing with their children.

Parents' affection must be shared—with one another and with their children. In the press of everyday life, it sometimes is hard to remember that each youngster in the family looks to his parents for the support and encouragement he needs. Parents are under pressure, too. They have a great deal to do and many responsibilities to carry. They tend to turn for help to the son or daughter they can count on at the time. They tend to avoid the unpleasant episodes precipitated by one of their children in favor of the more cooperative, compliant relationships in the family. They try to love all of their children fairly and impartially. The very idea of favoritism in their family is unpleasant. Yet it smolders beneath the surface in many a home, whether it is recognized or not.

Rivalry for parental love starts early in a child's experience. The firstborn has his parents all to himself for awhile. Then when a new baby arrives, "his nose is out of joint." He feels that the little newcomer has usurped his place in the family. He resents the time his parents give the new baby and does what he can to draw their attention to himself. His parents tell him that he should love his brother or sister, and he tries to but fails when he feels less favored. Then the green-eyed monster enters the picture, and he becomes more disagreeable than ever. This brings on his parents' disfavor, and he feels even more out of the picture.

Little children's impressions have a lasting effect in family relationships. Whether they are accurate or not, they are very real to a youngster. His jealousy of the sibling his parents seem to prefer cannot be dispelled by talk. He knows what he feels, and admonitions to love his brother only make him feel guilty that he does not. So he carries through the years the feeling that he is somehow unable to win his parents' favor. He is convinced that they love their other children more than they do him. This in spite of their assurance that they love all of their children the same.

Can Parents Love All Their Children Alike?

Many parents loudly assert that they love their children equally. Mothers and fathers generally feel that they should. They try not to play favorites among their children. They bend over backwards being fair. The very idea that one of their children is favored more than the others is repugnant to them. They are convinced that they do not play favorites, and that they love their children all alike.

Identical love is impossible. No one ever loves any two persons in exactly the same way. Each individual elicits his own special emotional response. This is especially true of children in the same family. Just the fact that one child is the oldest, and the other necessarily younger, makes a difference in the kind of love their parents feel for them. They expect more of their first child who is older. Their feeling for younger children is more relaxed because they have become accustomed to being parents by then. A sickly child receives the compassionate concern of his parents. The husky, happy one gets more their loving neglect. To do otherwise would be to ignore something essential in each.

A child who resembles some kinsman carries the image of that relative as part of his reputation. The youngster who early reminds his parents of some especially beloved member of the family walks in their favor, with no effort on his part. Another child with some of the characteristics of a black sheep in the family is penalized through no fault of his own. Because he looks like, talks like, walks like, or otherwise bears a resemblance to some relative, he is associated in the minds of his parents with that person—favorably or unfavorably. Since all the children in the family draw their genetic components from the same pool of inherited characteristics, family similarities frequently occur. What parents must remember is that one or more physical characteristics are not necessarily related to personality patterns or potentials. Just because a child has his grandfather's nose is no sign at all that he will be like the old man in other ways. Saddling a youngster with a ready-made set of expectations makes it hard for the child to find his own true identity. And, it increases the parents' difficulty in loving him for himself.

Some teens are easier to accept than others. Parents find tremendous differences in the way in which they guide their teenagers. One youngster is easy to raise. He or she listens to reason, is eager to please, and causes his or her parents little worry. Another teenager may be defiant, hard to reach, and generally difficult to understand. Mrs. Tanner has just about given up on her sixteen-year-old son. Twice this past year he has run away from home for short periods of time. His parents suspect him of using drugs. They feel helpless in their efforts to control his behavior. His father is away from home at his work most of the time, and his mother is beside herself with worry about the boy. At the end of her rope, Mrs. Tanner is considering sending her son to a military school in the hope that they can control him. The younger daughter is a comfort to her mother right now. Who is to say whether she is more compliant because she is more submissive or because she feels more accepted and understood by her parents?

Instead of insisting that they love all their children just alike, parents are wise to recognize their own honest feelings about each of their children. Only then can they give their children the special attention and acceptance each one needs. The simple truth is that children do not want to be loved just the same as the others in the family. Each needs his own special niche in his parents' life. Each wants to be appreciated and loved for himself and for what he or she is becoming. Each is different from the others, and should be accepted as uniquely lovable in his own right.

Discouraging Tattletales

Parents are in a quandary when one child in the family reports on another's behavior. They want to know what is going on and appreciate reliable reports on their children's behavior. But encouraging brothers and sisters to tell tales on one another is to set one child against another in the family. This is an all too familiar game children play with their teenage siblings. It rarely is fun for any member of the family and generally should be discouraged.

"Look what Janie's doing now!" This type of tattling is a youngster's bid for parents' favor by telling on a sister (or brother). Janie in this instance was experimenting with hair color for the first time. Her kid sister caught a glimpse of what was going on and dashed down the hall to tell their mother, "Guess what Janie's doing now . . . dying her hair!" Janie's mother first reaction was an explosive, "Oh no!" Then she saw the smug grin on the little tattler's face, and ignored the report. She did not want to encourage the younger daughter in telling on her sister, by rewarding her tale. Mother looked straight at her younger daughter and said, "Do you have your homework done, Dear?" Later when she was alone with Janie, they could discuss both the hair-coloring and the tattling in private. If Mother had not discouraged the tale-bearing, it might have meant many more unpleasant episodes between the two sisters.

Name-calling can be ignored, in most instances. When brothers and sisters become annoyed with one another, it is not unusual for them to resort to calling names of a derogatory type. The one insulted by the uncomplimentary name may run to either available parent to report the defamation of character. If the parents fail to make anything of the incident, the children usually settle the dispute "out of court." One mother we know says to the youngster who has been called an uncomplimentary name: "You know what your name is. You do not have to pay attention to any other." Later on when the dust settles, parent and name-caller can quietly discuss how childish name-calling is. This is particularly effective with teenagers ready to become more grown-up in dealing with younger brothers and sisters.

Teenagers' approval is important to younger children in the family. A boy looks up to his teenage brother and basks in his approval. When the older boy takes the time to encourage his younger siblings, they are less apt to pit themselves against him than if he ignores them. Name-calling and talebearing are reduced when younger children feel good about their teenage brothers and sisters. One way to discourage these unpleasant interactions is to build mutually satisfying relationships as much as possible. This is easier said than done, but it is worth the effort.

Should Teenagers Be Substitute Parents?

In many families a teenager helps the parents raise the younger children. As the oldest girl, a sister may have helped care for her younger siblings since she herself was little. She early was reminded that she was the oldest, and therefore, expected to be a good example. She has always been mother's little helper around the house and in looking after the children. When she finds this responsibility burdensome, she is apt to be impatient with her younger siblings. She may long to live her own life without having to be so responsible all the time. Just how much parents should expect of their older children in relationship to the younger ones in the family is a good question.

Must teenagers accept a tagalong? It looks so simple on the surface. The teenager is using the family car and a younger brother or sister wants to go along for the ride. It is too easy for one or both parents to insist that the teenager take the tagalong with him. In some situations this is acceptable. In others, the teenager may resent the younger child's presence. Parents have to be particularly perceptive of appropriate times to insist upon either the younger sibling's privilege or the older child's rights. Listening to what the situation means to the teenager helps in the decision. On some occasions a brother or sister is acceptable company, and in others not.

Brotherly love cannot be forced. Good rapport between children in the family is essential for their enjoying one another. If the teenager always has to cater to some younger sibling, he is apt to resent this burden. When a teenager enjoys the companionship of a younger brother or sister, he is far more willing to take his presence in good grace. Bo says, "I like to have my brother come along with me." The two boys have always been close. The younger fellow is good company but does not expect that Bo will always want him along. The two boys voluntarily have a number of joint projects going and share a number of friends as well as their parents with easy good humor. Their father believes that each son is entitled to live his own life without burdensome family obligations. Bo credits this parental philosophy with the mutual affection he and his younger brother have for each other.

Teenagers Want Their Own Things

One frequent family fuss is over violation of a teenager's right to have his things undisturbed by other members of the household. Parents generally recognize a teenager's need to have his own things unmolested by others. Younger brothers and sisters are not always so thoughtful.

Brothers and sisters who get into things belonging to a teenager are asking for trouble. This does not mean that the teenager is selfish or necessarily has anything to hide. It is not a question of deliberate poking in where they do not belong on the part of the other children in the family. It can be as simple as a youngster who needs a particular type of garment and knows where to find it—in another's closet. Mary Kay knew better than to borrow her sister's blouse without asking if she might. The two girls had shared one another's clothing before, so when Mary Kay was getting ready for a special affair she thought at once of her sister's new print blouse. She tried it on, and it was perfect for what she wanted right then. Unfortunately the blouse was torn and stained when Mary Kay returned it to her sister's rack. Her sister's angry reaction when the damage was discovered was immediately heard by the whole family. It took some diplomacy to rebuild the sisters' relationship that had been endangered by Mary Kay's impulsive behavior.

Diaries and letters are private papers. A teenager who keeps a diary enters into it his or her private, personal thoughts and experiences. Its very meaning is destroyed by any other's reading. Usually diaries are kept hidden and locked, but the hiding places can be found and the lock picked by an inquisitive family member. Then the fur is apt to fly far beyond the seeming importance of the offense. Members of a family do well to respect one another's personal property and privacy.

Parents' warnings are not as effective as their example. If Mother reads her children's mail, what she says about respecting another's property falls on deaf ears. Only when she sees to it that the person to whom a letter is addressed is the one to whom it is delivered unopened, can she enforce a family rule to that effect. Families generally have clearly understood policies guaranteeing each member's right to his or her personal correspondence. These practices are most important during the teen years when young people are struggling for a sense of self. Many teenagers are willing to share especially interesting letters in whole or in part with other members of the family, but only when they volunteer to and rarely when others pry.

Territorial imperatives among teenagers are obvious. Anthropologists have described how vigorously animals of various species fight for their territories. This is no less true of human teenagers, who struggle to have a place of their own, safe from the intrusion of other family members. In many families the home is large enough so that a teenager has a room of his own with a door that can be closed. In many other families the girls share a room, or brothers room together. Then it becomes imperative that the same-sex siblings respect each one's area that is his or hers alone. Even in a large family, sharing a crowded home, some personally private area—a box or a drawer at least, is required for each one. This fundamental need for a place to put one's keepsakes and the things one holds dear is not to be threatened in everyday life.

"It isn't fair!" a teenager shouts in protest when his or her parents consistently excuse a brother's or sister's intrusion into the teenager's life. The little "brat" who gets into a teenager's belongings, riffles his mail, or eavesdrops on the teenager's conversations is stepping out of line. He or she is expected to be disciplined by parents who are as much concerned for their teenager as for the younger child. When parents fail to protect the rights of one of their children and favor another unduly, they are accused of favoritism beyond what most teenagers can tolerate.

It is the younger child in the family who sometimes protests that the teenager gets all the breaks in the family. He or she feels left out of the family discussion about use of the family car, social life of high school, plans for college, and the more grown-up interests of parents and teenager. There is a frequent complaint that the teenager gets more money to spend, has more privileges, keeps later hours, and is less closely disciplined than are younger members of the family. Parents point out that the younger children will themselves be teenagers in time and that then they, too, will have some of the privileges of being older.

Most parents try to deal fairly with their children. This involves keeping in touch with what is going on, discovering how each of the youngsters feels about the situation, and eliciting their help in resolving the problem. As parents call for a showdown, not to mete out punishment, but to calm the troubled waters fairly, they gain their children's respect and build faith that issues will be settled equitably. This goes a long way toward establishing harmonious relationships among brothers and sisters in a family.

Coping with Quarreling

A home in which teenagers who do not quarrel with other members of the family is rare indeed. This is not to say that teenagers are naturally combative. It does assert that a certain amount of disagreement and fighting for one's rights is to be expected. The only families in which there is no fighting among the youngsters are those with an only child.

That someone feels short-changed is a safe assumption when quarreling breaks out at home. This is to be expected in any family in which there are things and people to be shared—the home and its furnishings, the car, the food, the television set, and most of all the parents' time and attention. Rightly or wrongly, the teenager or one of his brothers or sisters feels that he is not getting the rights and privileges to which he is entitled. It is possible that he carries a chip on his shoulder from a past experience and expects others to be more favored than he. It sometimes is a matter of attacking the sibling whose success is threatening at the time. Whatever the cause either current or ongoing, there are ways of coping with quarreling that work better than others. Parents and teenagers can learn more effective methods of dealing with difficulties as they begin to question their habitual approach to family fusses. Unfortunately, conventional efforts to reduce fighting among teenagers and children are relatively ineffective.

Don't try to find out who is right. The chances are that both of the adversaries feel justified in their positions. Each is entitled to his or her own opinions, feelings, and rights. Each fights for values and principles that are important from his point of view at the time. Attempts to judge the relative merits of either's case tend to be time-consuming and fruitless. By far, the better approach is to encourage both of the injured parties to express themselves as cooly as they can in an effort to state their own positions clearly and see where the issue is. Then, with some mutual understanding of what each is after, some reconciliation may be possible.

Finding out who started it is a waste of time. They probably both did in one way or another. The attacker may have precipitated the present incident, but that had a history in which the other was doubtless involved. Interpersonal quarreling usually builds up over a period of time with each baiting the other in covert ways. The tension increases until the aggressor lets the other have it, and the fight is underway. But, it did not begin with the first hostile word. Often the sweet little "innocent" in the situation is the provocateur, as many a teenager has discovered with his butter-wouldn't-melt-in-her-mouth younger sister. She may be after his attention, and when she can not win it by being pleasant, she provokes him into attacking her.

Treating all the children alike fails as often as not. Many parents try to reduce the rivalry among their children by giving them all the same treatment. They give identical gifts and attempt to discipline them in the same way. This may only increase the jealousy among the children. No two children can be guided in exactly the same manner. One is disciplined with a word, another requires more stringent methods. What pleases one child, annoys another. This is especially true when one or more of a family's children are teenagers. Then, it is important to recognize the increased stature and status of the teenager in ways that cannot be considered "kid stuff." Mr. Morton returned from a conference with identical gifts for his two daughters. The younger girl was delighted, the teenager was insulted. Their father accused his teenaged daughter of being ungrateful, and rubbed salt in her wound by commenting favorably on how nicely her sister had expressed her thanks for the same present. At which the older girl burst out: "That's just it, Daddy, I'm not a kid anymore, and I don't want you to treat me like one!"

Every teenager needs to feel special in his parents' eyes. Each child in the family wants to be recognized for his or her own particular qualities. A teenager busy at establishing a clear sense of his or her own identity looks to his parents for clues as to who he is and what kind of person he is becoming. Parents sense this when they comment favorably on some real effort that a teenager has put in on a project, regardless of how well it turned out. Their pleasure in a teenager's success and their understanding when he fails mean more than they may realize. One way to assure this happening more often than it does is to arrange for time alone with a teenager upon occasion.

Teenagers avoid whole family outings. They may have gone along quite happily the first dozen or so years of their lives. Then a day comes when a teenage son or daughter refuses to accompany the rest of the family on a holiday. This puzzles many a parent until the realization dawns that the time has come for more appropriate projects for parent and teenager. Then Father may invite his teenage son along with him on a fishing trip or to an out-of-town business and pleasure jaunt. Mother, similarly, may ask her teenaged daughter to go shopping with her, thereby enjoying both the girl's company and her good sense in consumer buying. Horizons must expand through the teen years. Travel should be to more distant places and experiences into more mature activities. Teenagers feel privileged as members of a family that provides for their maturing interests and tastes.

Welcome Favoritism

Not all favoritism in the family is regrettable. Now that we have reviewed the harm that unfortunate forms of family favoritism can do, let us turn to some of its more delightful aspects.

"You are my favorite granddaughter," grandmother says as she hugs the only girl in a family of five boys. The little girl wiggles with pleasure. When she becomes a teenager, she grins

sheepishly as she acknowledges the dubious compliment. Another family of blonds recently had an Oriental child with them for an extended period of time. The man of the house used to refer to the dark-eyed girl as "our favorite brunette." A mother of a six-foot-tall teenager in another household calls her son, "My favorite basketball player." These expressions of favoritism are acceptable because no one is hurt by them. There is no comparison implied. The person is given recognition as being special in ways that are welcome.

"My favorite wife" is the term of endearment that a thoughtful man uses in referring to his spouse. How much more acceptable this is than the worn phrases that are supposed to be amusing but that few women appreciate: "My old woman," "The wife," or "The Missus." One married woman we know responds to such an appellation with an amusing reference to her husband as "My former sweetheart." This lets him know that she loves him and at the same time that she prefers not be called his "old woman." There is something very special in the husband-wife relationship that should be acknowledged often. Children of all ages get a special sense of security from being frequently reminded that "Mama loves Papa" and that all is right with the marriage. Teenage Rodney jokes about his parents forming a coalition against him when he says, "What chance have I against such marital favoritism?"

Family loyalty is a fortunate form of favoritism. Members of a family want to feel that they are favored over outsiders. Their sense of closeness is a comfort to each person in the family. Their knowledge that the others in the family will stand back of them no matter what, provides them with a basic sense of security. Brothers may squabble among themselves from time to time. But let a stranger attack one of them, and he can count on his brothers to defend him. Parents may criticize their teenagers and children at home, but express their pleasure in their development to outsiders.

12
Winning with Teenagers

Some families are successful with their teenagers; others fail. The difference between winning and losing with teenagers in the family is in the way parents play their roles. When they are too heavy-handed they may win a point but lose the match with their young people. When they let their adolescents do as they will, the teenagers get their way in the immediate issue, but often lose their way in the long run. Only as parents and teenagers pull together in the family team can they hope to win.

Easygoing Parents Lose, Teens Win—Sometimes

When parents are overly-permissive with their teenagers, there is apt to be a chaotic atmosphere in the home. Neither generation is sure of where it stands. Both the older and the younger members of the family are unsure of themselves, and of one another. This makes for insecurity, even when the teenagers appear to be getting everything they want.

Teenagers seem to win the issue at stake when parents are too easygoing. Mother or father may make some mild objection, but back down rather than take a firm stand in seeing to it that their youngsters behave. The teenager scores in doing what he or she wants when he wraps his parents around his little finger. But this leaves him or her with a degree of uncertainty about himself, his parents, and what he is about to do. The young person often has a gnawing feeling that his parents may be right, so he feels guilty in not going along with what they have suggested. He secretly wishes his parents **155** would be firmer with him. This would give him something to push against as he declares his independence.

Parents are unsure of themselves and afraid to stand up to their teenagers at times. Their uncertainty serves to increase their feeling of inadequacy, so they are under double jeopardy. Because they are overly-permissive, they "let their teenagers get away with murder." Then when the kids get into trouble, the parents as well as the youngsters suffer. One mother we know says, "I know I am too easy on my kids. I let them do things that are harmful now and might become even more serious. But the trouble is, I am not sure myself of when to put down my foot and when to ease up on the pressure."

No one wins when there are no rules. Overly-permissive families are often in an uproar because there is no sense of direction in the home. The kids run wild, like the boys in Golding's *Lord of the Flies*, until someone is injured. In the meantime, everyone has been hurt. The parents by not having peace, quiet, and a sense of order in their lives; and the children by having no protection from their wildest impulses. The youngsters end up being spoiled brats, and the parents are left with a feeling of exhausted failure. Every game has to have some rules, or no one knows who wins or what the next play should be.

Get-Tough Parents Seem to Win While Teens Lose

Families ruled by an iron fist appear neat and orderly on the surface. Authoritarian parents seem to run things their own way. They lay down the law, and see to it that the kids obey. They brook no nonsense and hear few if any appeals. Their teenagers either conform or get out. They lose an argument with parents who allow no questioning of their authority.

Father cannot always be right. He may boss and bluster, but no man can be right all the time, about every issue. So poor Dad gets "egg on his face" when he poses as the family dictator, no matter how benevolent. Then he either eats humble pie or refuses to admit that he has erred. He is stuck with a ridiculous position that he cannot maintain. He loses the respect of his teenagers by insisting that they honor his position—right or wrong. If he is blind to what he is doing, he lives in a fool's paradise. When he becomes aware of the empty authority he wields at home, he is bereft of his power and has already lost the close companionship of his family.

Mother does not always know what's best. She gets away with the illusion that she knows what is best for her children when they are small. But as they become teenagers, they challenge her omniscience. If she insists that she knows what young people should do and how, she finds that they no longer look to her for guidance. When she takes over any decision on which she is consulted, she soon finds that fewer and fewer questions are brought to her. She is left alone with her wisdom, hardly a winner in anyone's eyes.

Teenagers are expert in their own fields. They know their peers and other members of the younger generation far better than their parents can. They understand what "all the other kids" are doing or wearing or saying. They know how they feel as young people, better than even the wisest parent can guess. They see how things look to them, which is not always the way they appear to other members of the family. One of the tragedies of the autocratic family is that teenagers' expertise is not utilized. Much as Hitler drove brain-power out of Nazi Germany, parents who act like dictators alienate their brightest youngsters. So the victory the parents seem to have won is an empty one when the parent-teenager tie has been broken.

Problem-Solving Families Win

Everybody wins in the family that has learned how to pull as a team. Parents and teenagers are not on opposite sides of an issue. They work together toward a mutually agreeable solution to any problem that comes up. This does not happen suddenly as sons and daughters become teenagers. It is a way of living together that develops over the years. Even while youngsters are very young they can be given a voice in matters that concern them in the family. Gradually over the years they participate in more and more family discussions. By the time the teen years arrive, members of the family are old hands at facing decisions with a united front.

They attack the problem, rather than one another. Some families seem to be in a constant state of war. For, every issue finds the family members squared off opposite each other. Then, whoever wins the scrimmage, emerges a loser because of the failure the others feel. Winning families, on the other hand, attack the problem confronting them together. They focus first on what the issue at stake is. They listen to how the several family members feel about it. They welcome suggestions for its solution. They choose the route that appears most feasible to them all. Then, as further questions arise, they are aired and met in turn. Voices may be raised as each one makes his or her point. But, because the focus is on the search for a workable solution, the family members themselves do not feel that they are under attack.

Creative energy is released when tangles are unravelled together. One minister's family we know follows the church's method of resolving issues by brainstorming. It started the year Cindy took a shorthand course. She started to record family meetings and transcribe her notes for the others. Participation picked up when the children discovered that what they said would appear in typescript. Then, when someone suggested that they brainstorm for vacation possibilities, the ideas rained in on Cindy so fast her pencil flew over her stenographic pad. The list of suggestions posted on the family bulletin board was impressive and served as a basis for planning over the next several weeks. Parents and teenagers brought home brochures and gave reports on what could be found at more than a dozen of the vacation spots proposed. When the time came for the family vote on their vacation site, the brainstorming had paid off in familiarizing each of the family members on the various possibilities. Everyone agreed that year's vacation was the best ever, partly because of the joint creativity that went into its planning.

Each one becomes more self-directing in the problem-solving group approach. All members of the family are encouraged to express themselves. Each speaks for himself in consort with the others of the family. This is especially helpful in focusing what it is that a given situation means to the others. It is valuable for a family's teenager to sharpen his sense of who he is and what he wants enough to put his goals into words. This develops his sense of self-direction. It is an incentive toward being more independent. So, one result of the problem-solving approach in families is to help develop each member's sense of identity and direction.

Cooperating with one another is a key to success in the family. Rather than compete for attention and privileges, the emphasis is on cooperating so that everyone may benefit. The Williams family decided late one afternoon to have a picnic. Mrs. Williams was not sure that she could get everything together soon enough to give them time for a real family outing. Teenage Sam and Sue rallied the rest of the family by volunteering to make the sandwiches and prepare the fruit punch. Mother whipped up a quick loaf cake while Dad serviced the car. The two younger children got out the picnic basket and packed the right number of plates, cups, napkins, and other essentials. In twenty minutes the Williams family was enroute to their favorite picnic spot. As Mrs. Williams said, "We'd have never made it without everyone pitching in to make it possible."

Most families cooperate in a crisis. Let Dad break his ankle or Mother get a virus, and the whole family meets the critical situation with courage. It is in the little everyday things that many a family has to learn to pull together. When Mother has a let down in spirit, it is a perceptive teenager who can give her the TLC she needs. When Dad's injury is to his ego rather than to his ankle, his family can help him rebuild his confidence only when they are responsive to his mood. This is the acid test of cooperation in the family.

Communication Goes Both Ways

It is easy to sound off when you feel that some injustice is being done. It is somewhat harder to listen carefully to someone else's complaint. If you live in a winning family, both transmitters and receivers are kept in good working order so that each member can get through to the others without too much static.

Parent-teen static is to be expected in family communication. It is during the teen years that the young people in the family are struggling to assert themselves. In their efforts to become autonomous persons, they sometimes come on stronger than they had meant. They say things that sound rude and rebellious to their parents. This turns off many a mother and father who retreat in disappointment or flare up at their teenagers self-protecting defense. The other pitfall is quite as painful. Youngsters who once confided in their parents now take their confidences elsewhere. A girl friend now is consulted more often than Mother. Some best friend outside the family almost seems to take the place of the parents as confidantes. Noisy interference and the silent treatment are related problems in parent-teenager communication. The tendency is to retreat into silence when one does not feel that he is being heard with sympathetic understanding.

Parents are open and honest with their teenagers when lines of communication are kept open. They do not waste time protecting a shaky ego. They set a good example of admitting mistakes as they occur so that the family can get on to more important issues and answers. Don, Senior, apologized to Junior for poor judgment in last weekend's flair-up. Junior grinned, and accepted his father's apology with good grace, saying, "That's all right Dad, we all make mistakes." How different the relationship between the two men if the older had stood on his dignity as the father of the family and refused to admit that he had been wrong! Rather than bringing the two closer together, they would have been driven farther apart. Few things are quite so helpful to teenagers as parents who acknowledge their imperfections.

Teenagers dare to admit their mistakes when parents do not try to be perfect. They waste little energy in coverups or deception. They have learned from their parents' example that the quickest way out of a mess is to make a clean breast of it, and get what help is needed in making amends. Teenagers naturally make mistakes, as all persons do. They are confronted with many situations in which they are inexperienced, and so must learn in action what works and what does not. If their parents come down like a ton of bricks, the kids learn not to expose themselves to successive tirades. They clam up and then their parents wonder why their teenagers do not confide in them anymore. One of the surest ways to keep communication open in a family with teenagers is not to be too upset when things are not perfect. Perfectionists are hard to live with, and they make life difficult for themselves in expecting too much of others.

Anything can be shared at any time in an open family. Each member knows that whatever has happened can be discussed and worked through together. This is easy when the event to be shared is a happy occasion to be celebrated. Harder by far is having to relate something that will discredit the family or bring on displeasure. Andy "lost" his report card rather than having to show such poor grades to his parents. Having no report card for the school records brought Andy to the principal's attention where his poor marks as well as his carelessness in losing his report card compounded his problem. Fortunately the principal was an understanding man, sensed what a spot Andy was in, and volunteered to help Andy make things right with his parents and with his teachers. His compassion for Andy's plight gave the boy the confidence he needed to retrieve the "lost" report card. His offer to get a tutor to help with the courses Andy had to have helped square things at home. When Andy's father discovered what was happening, he encouraged his son to drop one of his electives, and devote himself to the courses in which he was being tutored. The family stood back of Andy in his struggle to improve his grades, and later laughed over how they had missed Andy's first cry for help. A family slogan in attempted cover-ups thereafter was: "What's the matter? Lose your report card?"

Hazards to Be Avoided

The things people do without thinking can make life complicated for those they live with as well as for themselves. In few times of life is this more true than when there are teenagers in the family. Then, out of their eagerness to have everything right for their young people, parents "just naturally" say and do the very things that make things worse.

Nagging, scolding, and warning a teenager are rarely happy ways of helping. Yet, out of their concern for their youngsters, parents sometimes drift into just such unpleasant habits. One parent or the other keeps after a sluggish teenager in an effort to get him or her to do what is expected of him. The nagging is apt "to bug" the young person to the place where he either avoids the nagging parent or turns a deaf ear in that direction. Scolding a youngster is quite ineffective in correcting his mistakes. The chances are that the teenager knows quite as well as do his parents that he has stepped out of line. He has to want to improve himself before there will be any real change in his behavior. Warning a child of any age does not work unless it is accompanied with clear-cut reasons of what the danger consists, and feasible ways of avoiding its hazards.

Dora is at a particularly rebellious stage. So much so that anything her parents forbid she wants to do. They have tried to warn her against frequenting a questionable hangout. But in her defiance, she continues to go there. She has been so turned off by her parents' continual efforts to "baby" her that their warning but drives her ever further into possible trouble. At the moment her grandmother is the only adult she will listen to, possibly because Granny calmly talks over with her how to cope with her overly-protective parents and her own rebellious nature. In the course of these discussions, the older woman has given her granddaughter some real help in dealing with some of the difficult situations Dora faces.

Probing and prying into a teenager's affairs is self-defeating more often than not. At this stage of life a young person hotly defends his privacy. He resents any intrusion into his personal relationships. He or she vigorously protects his private papers from others' eyes and flares into outraged indignation when he finds evidence of prying. Seth had been saving money for weeks for a birthday present for his girl friend. Because it was more expensive than his mother might approve, he kept the gift and its cost a secret from her. Then one day when she was cleaning his room, she found the jeweler's sales slip at the bottom of his drawer. An angry scene ensued between mother and son, each both mad and hurt by the other. The result was an even wider gulf between Seth and his parents.

Preaching is out of place in the family. What is expected in church on Sunday morning is not acceptable that evening at home. Pointing out a moral and preaching at teenagers usually turns them off. They do not like being lectured for things they should not have done or reminded of what they have left undone. They generally feel that judging their behavior usurps them of their rights to make such evaluations themselves. By the time a boy and girl reach the teen years they can be expected to know right from wrong. When their behavior falls short, they know it, most of the time. They do not need to have their misdeeds served up as texts for family sermons. They writhe at having their motives questioned by parents who do not know all the facts. Most of all they do not like to be psychoanalyzed by family members any more than other people do. Such parental methods tend to weaken their relationships with their teenagers. They are clearly hazards to be avoided, whenever possible.

Coping with Conflict

Conflict is inevitable in a family with teenagers. The two generations grew up in different times and see things from differing points of view. Because parents care about their maturing young people, they try to guide them as they see fit. Teenagers, on the other hand, are desperately trying to become independent persons in their own right. Something has to give in the tug-of-war between parents and teenagers. It helps to know how to handle the normal pulling and hauling that goes on in day to day living in the family.

Knowing where to expect friction is helpful in avoiding it at times. When a teenager understands what upsets a parent, disturbing episodes sometimes can be circumvented. Knowing one's own young people well enough to anticipate what upsets them is a first step in dealing with difficulties with them. Emmy is a good student. She has developed good study habits over the years that have served her well. She usually does her homework as soon as she gets home from school on Friday afternoon so that she will have her weekend free for family and friends. Emmy's parents know this and approve. But, recently Emmy's mother has interrupted her study with a series of trivial requests and questions that have caused the two women to flare up at one another. They both feel right in what they have done. But, Emmy's mother now sees that it might have been better to respect Emmy's good study habits enough not to break into them with inconsequential interruptions.

Jon has learned that when his mother has one of her sinus headaches, it is no time to make unusual requests of her. She comes down to breakfast in the morning with her face screwed up in pain and with no interest in food or conversation. There is little that Jon or his father can do to relieve her misery except to express their sympathy and make things as easy for her as possible. If Jon needs his sweatshirt washed on such a day, he quietly does it himself rather than upset his mother with one thing more than she can undertake.

Planning ahead to avoid issues is one way to avoid conflict in the family. The first time that Viola brought a new boy-friend home, her parents were polite while the boy was present, but as soon as he had gone, her father criticized him in ways Viola considered unreasonable and unjust. She and her mother talked over the episode and undertook to prepare Viola's father for other fellows she brought home. Viola was careful to tell her folks something about a new boyfriend before his first visit to her home. Her mother talked over with her father how fine it was that Viola wanted to bring her friends home to meet her parents. She discovered that her husband was finding it hard to let his only daughter grow up enough to have suitors. So, from then on, Viola was careful to give her father his full share of her attention before, during, and after a boy-friend's visit. In time, Viola's father was proud of his daughter's popularity and appreciated all she and her mother did to make it a little easier for him to accept rivals for his daughter's attention with good grace.

Acknowledging responsibility early is helpful in keeping issues to a minimum. Deceit, coverup, and refusal to accept blame for some unfortunate occurrence compounds a conflict more often than not. Immediate assumption of responsibility for an unfortunate incident can be and often is quite disarming. Al came home with the family's new car that he had taken on an errand for his mother. He crawled on his hands and knees into the family room where his parents were watching television. His mother laughed and said, "What on earth are you doing down on the floor?" Al barked like a dog and replied, "I'll soon be in the dog house, so I thought I'd practice up." He went on to confess that the new car had a "dimple" in the rear fender where he had backed into a low post at the shopping center. "Not a soul in sight to blame but me," he confessed. What might have been an ugly scene became a good-humored acceptance of the dented fender because of Al's ng and prompt admission of what had happened.

ling alternative ways out of potential unpleasantness is
the effort in avoiding conflict. Everyone has off days
now and then. When people feel out of sorts, they take out
their feelings on one another unless they have learned better
ways of expressing their negative emotions. Mrs. Long used
to fly off the handle whenever her teenagers annoyed her.
She excused her quick temper by saying that she was just
like her mother who flared up in anger when she was a girl.
In a group counseling program at church, she found herself
acknowledging that she did not like her behavior any more
than she had her mother's. She resolved to change her ways,
and got the group's support in finding alternatives to venting
her bad temper on her family. She used her son's punching
bag whenever she found her anger mounting and let the ball
have it in all its fury. Other parents, and teenagers, too, find
music, or sports, or meditation, or prayer valuable alternatives
to destructive behavior in the family.

Enriching the Environment

Some problems can be solved by expanding the horizons
for the family or any of its members. Monotonous routines
create problems in many a family with teenagers. Young people in the second decade of life are eager for new experiences.
They like to travel, to see new people, and to try out new
ways of doing things. Alert parents can provide for these needs
of youth by a variety of ways.

Special trips, travel, and plans add to the vitality of a family
at any age. When there are teenagers in the home, they are
invaluable. Lou, a senior in high school, has been applying
for scholarships at a number of colleges across the country.
Last week he received a favorable reply from a university
with which his family had had no previous contact. With the
holiday weekend coming up, Lou's father suggested that they
pile into the family camper and go look over the campus.
Lou was thrilled and asked if he could take his chum who

was also interested in the college along, too. The camper had a good work-out that weekend with four adults in it, but they all had a grand time and decided that the trip was well worth the time and gas it took.

Many plans must be laid well in advance. When Chris's Spanish teacher suggested that he might serve as an exchange student in South America, he and his family explored the possibility for weeks. His parents encouraged Chris in the venture and helped him earn some of the extra money he would need for his year away from home. Such a venture cannot be undertaken on impulse. It requires whole family planning to work but is usually well worth the effort.

Special projects kindle problem-solving potential in a family. If they are big enough to challenge a teenager, they can vitalize his or her participation in family activities. Gerri had been campaigning for a recreation room where she could entertain her friends. It was an expensive project with commercial bids too high for the work to be done. Gerri and her folks looked into the possibility of doing the work themselves over weekends and in the evenings when they could spare the time. Gerri scouted around and found good quality paneling at a reasonable price. Her mother discovered a floor covering on sale that could be laid easily. Gerri's older brother volunteered to install acoustical tile on the ceiling. Her mother recovered furniture and painted a refrigerator she was no longer using to equip the room. The project kept the family busy for months and was a valuable addition to their home. When the last tile was laid, Gerri grinned at her folks and said, "Well that's done, now what will we do?"

Whole-family functioning beyond itself is enrichment with stretches in it. When everyone in a family gets involved in a project beyond itself, something wonderful happens. Each member is alive to the potentials of the activity underway. Family talk is quickened by all the details of their planning and work. Teenagers and parents find one another as persons as they function together side by side. There is nothing like throwing oneself into service to others, especially when the giving can be in conjunction with others in the family.

The Rosses have been devoting their Saturdays in recent weeks to cleaning and refurbishing facilities for indigent elders across town. It all came about when Cille was doing volunteer work in that area. She gave several hours a week after school to reading to aging men and women whose sight was failing. Sometimes she ran errands for them, on other days she was asked to write a letter for some older person whose hands were too crippled with arthritis to hold a pen. Cille became interested in these old folks and from time to time brought other members of her family over to visit the granny she had "adopted."

It was when Mr. Ross saw the peeling paint on Granny's woodwork that he asked her if she would mind his touching it up the next time he came to see her. Her face glowed with pleasure when she proudly showed her neighbors her newly painted room. In time the whole Ross family got involved in redoing others' rooms, too. This led to the redecorating of their living room, and even the installation of a used television set that Junior put into good working order. The Ross family was recently cited for their community improvement project, recognition that was merited but unsought. Their own satisfaction in giving themselves to others was reward enough.

Many families do other things in projects beyond themselves. The Moores are busy campaigning for their favorite political candidates. The Thomases have thrown themselves into a home mission project for their church. The Seeleys are active in a local ecology project that takes much of the leisure time of every member of the family. "The nice thing about having teenagers is that you can do so many things together when your children get old enough to work right along with you," says Mrs. Seeley. She might have added that such a winning combination is the result of outgoing spirit and happy interaction within and beyond the family.

13
Telling It Like It Feels

"Tell it like it is!" has become a slogan of youth in search of candor. Today's teenagers tend to look for honesty; they react against the phoniness they see around them. They say they want to face the facts as they see them. Many adults, too, have had enough of deception and coverup. The quest of the latter decades of the twentieth century may well be for truth.

Emotional integrity is an important facet of honest interaction. It means being candid with one another as to one's own inner feelings. It involves identifying one's emotions and sharing one's feelings with one another. This is not an easy task for persons of any age. It is particularly difficult for teenagers whose emotions are hard to describe, difficult to name, and complicated to share.

How It Feels to Be Young

Young people do not find it easy to put their feelings into words. They experience so many emotions, in such new and confusing ways that they hardly know themselves what it is that they feel. Ask an upset teenager how he feels, and he often is hard put to answer you directly. He is too busy sorting out his own confusions to put a label on his inner turmoil.

Confused and searching is the way some teenagers describe their emotional climate. Life opens up so rapidly for young people that they have difficulty assimilating it. They grow up so fast, they are overwhelmed by feelings they have not felt before, experiences they have not known before, rela- **169** tionships they have not had before. No wonder they swing from excited exuberance to confused frustration.

Teenagers, like many of us of other ages, are groping painfully for a new way of life that will satisfy their longing. When adults around them are unsure, it becomes increasingly difficult for teenagers to know who they are, whither they are going, and how and why. As one articulate teenager puts it: "The world looks upon us as children; we strive to see the world as adults. A constant struggle thus ensues. This is confusion."

Alive in every fiber of being is often felt by healthy young people. They tell of thrilling to the sense of being vitally, exuberantly alive. Alive when they laugh until the tears come and cry until they can cry no more. They feel love as a caress or as a blinding stab to their very core. They speak of physical exhilaration and the thrill of exercise that leads to victorious accomplishment.

Eager to be in tune with the universe is a feeling that emerges from the surge of life within youth. Many a young person today wants to live close to nature, to respond to the cycle of the seasons, and to protect the earth and growing things around him. Youth join with adults in movements concerned with ecology, water and air purification, and the preservation of living things. They want to know all kinds of people at work, at play, in suffering, and in rejoicing. Many would rather not be protected from pain and aging and death because these too are part of life. Teenagers tend to see life as a privilege, and many are responsive to its challenge.

Feeling guilty is a frequent experience of the teen years. Youth is a time of life when one is rarely satisfied with oneself even when others do not complain. Aspirations are high, and performance lags behind in many instances. A teenager feels guilty when he fails to come up to what his parents expect of him, and he feels remorse when he lets himself down. When he stretches away from his family in an effort toward independence, he feels guilty at having hurt his parents in the process. If he conforms to their wishes in every way, he stifles his own urge to become autonomous which is equally upsetting. "I spend half my time trying to make amends for something I did that I should not have done, or making up for things I should have done and didn't," says Amanda. The pushing of impatient adults only increases the guilt feelings of sensitive young people.

How Parents Discourage Teenagers

Parents discourage their teenagers when they are overprotective. It is easy for a mother to smother her children with her well-meaning concern for their safety. It is fairly normal for a father to want to protect his sons from the buffeting he has had. Almost any Dad yearns to keep his daughter the sweet little girl he doted on when she was a child. Now that she is a teenager, he is critical of her boyfriends and resistant of her efforts to be grown-up and sophisticated. These are understandable parental responses to their maturing children, but they are discouraging nevertheless.

Overly protective parents seem to try to keep their teenagers from growing up. They are so afraid that their youngsters will be harmed by the world as it is that they surround them with protective concern. Too many rules and regulations keep a teenager from flexing his own muscles and making his own choices. The boy struggles to free himself from the warm little nest his parents have built for him. The girl resists being treated like a child and gets discouraged when she lacks the strength to win her freedom.

Ruthie is easily discouraged. She gives up any effort in which she is not immediately successful. She refuses to try anything that looks the least bit difficult. Her teachers say that she is bright enough but appears to lack the will to work. Ruthie herself does not know what is the matter. She has come to believe what she has heard over and over from her mother: "You are making a mess of that. Give it to me to finish for you." It all started when Ruthie was still a little girl. Her mother used to take the scissors from her because she might cut herself. Her crayons were removed because she colored over the lines in her picture book. When she tried to sew, her stitches were not even so her mother finished her apron for her. Now in her teens, Ruthie is convinced that her mother can do everything better than she can. So, she hangs back, afraid to fail, fearful of trying, overprotected to the point of immobility.

Parents who expect too much discourage their teenagers. There are some parents who seem never to be satisfied with their teenagers. When Carter's report card showed marked improvement over the last marking period, his father was reluctant to note his progress. Instead he said, "Still room for improvement in Math, isn't there, Son?" Carter's dad may have meant well. Perhaps he was trying to motivate his son to keep on improving his grades. But the net effect that Carter felt was discouragement at not being able to satisfy his father no matter how well he did.

Parents criticize their teenagers because they care about them. They want their sons and daughters to be a credit to the family. They would like them to appear well, both when they leave the house and while they are at home. They wish their youngsters could be well-mannered, highly motivated, helpful in the family, and well thought of by their neighbors. This is a lot to expect of a teenager who has his own goals and interests. So, most parents do not have to look far to find plenty of things about their teenagers to criticize.

Parental criticism expresses itself in many ways. Some comes forth in a steady stream of suggestions, admonitions, and why-don't-you-isms. Some mothers give their teenagers the silent treatment of implied criticisms so clear that they cannot be ignored. Other parents vent their annoyance in angry accusations. Loud and unpleasant as such attacks may be, they are sometimes easier for a teenager to take than those which are more restrained. A teenager can meet the shouted command in kind. He or she can match the shrill criticism in a noisy conflict of wits heard in many a family.

Teenagers Are Critical

The teen years are a critical time of life. Studies show that most teenagers are critical of the things and people around them. When they get together after school, they are critical of their teachers, the school and its rules, and of the way other kids behave. When they reach home, they sound off against their brothers and sisters and take out their critical ill-humor on whomever is handy. Some of this comes from the habit of being hard to please over the years. Some comes from the inner turmoil teenagers feel. Much derives from teenage idealism that not yet has been tempered by reality.

Criticizing home and its furnishings is frequent among young teenagers. It is as though as childish ways are outgrown, a young person begins to cast off the things he has had around him. These are the years when a teenager campaigns for a new car, new furnishings for the house, and among the boldest, even for a new home or neighborhood.

Objecting to family practices comes into its own in the teen years. Little children may go along with family customs without question. But, teenagers often challenge them. "Why do I have to go visit Aunt Clara again this Sunday afternoon?" asks Delia with petulance. For years the whole family has called on the mother's invalid sister every Sunday. Now Delia has other things to do and objects to being expected to go along with the rest of the family on their weekly visit.

Teenagers voice their objection to many ways that have been taken for granted before. Each must be met in turn by most families with young people. Some objections can be conceded as reasonable; others are too important to relinquish; and still others can be compromised in family discussion.

Criticism of family members by teenagers is well nigh universal. Teenagers sound off about their brothers and sisters for all sorts of real and imagined offenses. Younger siblings get into teenagers' belongings and into their hair. Older brothers and sisters are bossy and overbearing according to many a teenage boy or girl. At times there seems to be little that their brothers and sisters can do that will please an irritable teenager.

Parents, too, are actively criticized by teenagers in many instances. As young people prepare themselves for leaving home, they seem to try to convince themselves that they can manage quite well without their families. For years before teenagers are ready to be completely independent, they push off from their families with gestures of autonomy that often take on the guise of criticism. Without this critical thrust toward independent living, teenagers would find it hard to leave the parental nest.

Constructive Criticism

If it is good to "tell it like it feels" and not keep one's true feelings concealed, how then does one express the criticisms that surge up within one during the teen years? So much criticism in the family is corrosive and hurtful that most family members agree that it should be held to a minimum. How best to do this is worth considering in theory and in practice.

Putting anger into words that express one's feelings is often a help. When another person has been annoying, it is easy to blast forth with a torrent of angry criticism of him and his behavior. Far more effective is putting into expressive language the rage that one feels. Our mother tongue is rich with possibilities for labeling one's mad moments. One can be annoyed, irritated, aggravated, exasperated, provoked, indignant, enraged, furious. You can smolder, boil, flare up, or explode with anger. Going into the vernacular you can fly off the handle, blow your stack, blow your top, hit the ceiling, or even "go bananas." When another's behavior has been upsetting, one recourse is to express your feeling verbally, "I sizzle with rage when this happens."

Criticizing without personal attack is to be recommended. Granted, criticism in the family is warranted many times and has its beneficial aspects. Keeping it from being needlessly painful is a worthy goal. Anything that directly attacks another person is apt to be harmful. It is not necessary to strike him physically to hurt him. Striking at his ego can be even more painful. Attributing unworthy motives to another individual is an attack upon him. Telling a teenager, "You meant to be mean," is a blow below the belt. His retort, "You don't try to understand," is a counterattack in kind.

Pointing out preferences can be constructive. When Sadie had come late to dinner again, her mother let her know how she felt. She said: "Sadie, when you are late it upsets me. I'd rather you'd tell me when you know you will have to be later than usual so that I'll know what to expect." She did not tell her daughter that she was thoughtless and irresponsible. She simply expressed her preference for handling a similar situation in the future.

Ernie did not want to hurt his mother's feelings when she cleaned up his cluttered room, but he had to let her know that he did not want her poking into his things when he was away. So, he told his mother: "Thanks, Mom for clearing that mess in my room. But if you don't mind, I'll do it myself from now on. I've got to eventually and I might as well start now." His mother beamed her approval, and the crisis was averted.

Building up the other's self-confidence keeps criticism constructive. Making an effort to express appreciation at the same time that some suggestion for improvement is given makes the implied criticism more effective. Joe had used his father's precious compost on the garden path where its value would be lost. Dad put his arm across Joe's shoulder in a man to man gesture as he expressed his appreciation for the boy's help. He told his son how fine it was to be able to count on Joe to work along with him in the garden. He asked if Joe would like to help build a new compost heap with clippings from the lawn. Together the men talked about the value of recycling organic material. Joe developed an appreciation for what his father was trying to do, at the same time that he got the message about reserving the compost for mulching the garden.

Sometimes one can use the sandwich approach for getting a suggestion over to another individual in a constructive way. First comes a well-deserved compliment on whatever the person has done well. Then comes a proposal for improvement in some detail. Finally a smile of approval and some expression of pride in the person, the relationship, or both.

Ella's little brother adores her. Ella has won that admiration by going out of her way to build up the little guy's confidence in himself whenever she can. Early one evening when Ella had finished her practicing, she went out-of-doors to find her car lumpy with paste wax and her little brother wet with perspiration in his effort to rub it smooth. Her exclamation of pleasure at having her car waxed made her brother stretch up to his full height. He beamed as he told her how clean he had gotten the car before he started the wax job. Her next move was the critical one, "How about letting me help with the rubdown?" she asked. Together they worked away until the car shone. "Now, let's show it off as we run down for a soda," was her suggestion. At the corner they met a favorite neighbor to whom Ella called out, "Look what a grand wax job my handsome brother here gave my car." Ella may never make the diplomatic corps, but she has learned a basic principle of human relations—build up the other fellow.

Maturing Emotionally

Growing up emotionally takes years of conscious effort and encouragement. It is one of the most important goals of healthy family living. It is basic in open, candid, and supportive communication of feelings in a family. Without it the members of the household go about in emotional turmoil. Like a baby who gets red in the face and throws himself around when he is angry or the toddler who expresses his rage in a temper tantrum, emotionally immature adults and teenagers explode with feelings they cannot express appropriately.

Emotional maturity is being able to: (1) relate consistently to others with mutual support and fulfillment; (2) find as much satisfaction in giving as in receiving; (3) be free from chronic tensions or anxieties; (4) be flexible and able to adjust to change; (5) cope creatively with things and persons as they are; (6) express constructively one's potentially hateful feelings (which all individuals have to some extent from time to time); and (7) love widely and deeply in ways that enrich and bless. You may have still others to suggest. However emotional maturity is defined, it implies an important truth—emotional development can stop at an immature level. Physical growth and development proceeds to maturity with little personal effort. Emotional health is an achievement both for the person and for the family.

Teenagers strive toward maturity throughout the second decade of their lives. They stretch up and fill out as budding young adults. They grow intellectually as they enjoy learning and knowing. They find themselves philosophically as their values and concerns mature. They blossom spiritually as they realize that they are truly children of God. They mature emotionally as they interact in ever more grown-up ways with other persons. Their first and most lasting lessons in emotional maturing take place within their homes as they try to behave as the older, wise members of their families do. This is a precious gift of parents to their sons and daughters—to model the good and the right for their children.

Parents, too, are maturing. As long as they live, they are either repeating the unhappy patterns of their past, or they are developing newer and better ways of living. Butch Patterson went into periodic rampages in which his children cowered with fear. His purple rages were violent, much as his father's had been before him. In his calm moments he regretted having lost his temper, but he continued in his wild outbursts until his wife threatened to leave him if he did not control himself. Contrite, he said he would try to restrain his temper tantrums if his wife would help him. She did so by tipping him off as the first signs of an angry outburst appeared. Then she would grin at him, shake her head, and softly say, "Oh, oh, here we go again."

At this reminder, Butch would stop cold in the middle of a sentence, and change his stance. He found that it helped to breathe deeply, get a drink of cold water, go out for a fast walk, or get into some physical activity at once until his emotional temperature returned to normal. His son, who had trembled in fear as a little child, now began to admire his father's effort to mature emotionally. Together the two men of the family agreed that sounding off like an ill-bred youngster was too immature for men of their stature.

Families encourage maturity of feeling when they provide an emotionally healthy climate. They encourage their members to level with one another. They withhold making judgments of one another in critical ways. They do not deal harshly with a member who has made a mistake, has admitted it, and is trying to make amends. They believe so much in the forgiveness of sins that they are compassionate with one another. They readily acknowledge their weaker moments and attempt to learn from them. They express their love for each other in ways that help each member feel strong and confident most of the time. They let sorrow be expressed without having to put up a brave front within the family. They mourn with the bereft and rejoice with the victorious even in little every-day things. They accept their own honest feelings as they arise and express them in mutually fulfilling ways.

Such families are rarely citadels of silence. They ring with laughter as they rejoice together. Their members call out to one another to observe a sunset or watch a falling star. They noisily work through their conflicts until the contending parties are content. They throw themselves into whatever has to be done with wit and willingness. They let life surge through them, between them, and within them, because they are not afraid to feel.

14
Living and Loving in the Family

Living and loving are both homemade. Each person literally learns to live within his or her home. Every one grows up reflecting the love within his family. Living and loving go together, you cannot have one without the other, in the fullest sense. Children growing up in loveless homes are forlorn, neglected, and stunted in their development. Teenagers who have known the warmth of their parents' caring through the first dozen or more years of their lives are usually full of life and love for others. They have learned how to live lovingly as surely as they have learned how to speak their mother tongue—by growing up in its atmosphere and its application day after day through their formative years.

The Emotional Climate of Your Home

Some homes are quietly formal and precise, others are vigorously informal, even hectic. Some families are watchful of each member's going and comings, others are more casual about their supervision. Some families are carefully quiet and restrained, others are noisily involved in living, playing, and getting things done. Some parents and teenagers function as a team with each supporting and encouraging the others. In still other homes, the members go their separate ways, independent of one another.

Living together is more than shared space in your family; it is its pattern of interaction that makes your home what it is. Living in a family means the possibility of creating together a sense of unity that provides a foundation for all **179** of life. Interaction at the deepest levels gives each member a feeling of being understood and appreciated. Feeling cared for, a teenager can relax and grow with fulfillment and satisfaction.

"She's growing up just like her mother," is a compliment both to his wife and their winsome daughter. The teenage girl is pleased and proud of her father's approval and of his observation that she is becoming more and more like her mother whom she admires. Feeling at ease with both her parents, she is free to assert herself in ways unlike her mother's. Because of her warm acceptance in the family, she can go forth and be herself. "Like-father-like-son" gives a lad a unique expression of kinship. He may rebel from such a close tie at times, but the sense of mutual approval warms and encourages him nonetheless.

Purr words and slur words give a clue to the emotional climate of a family. This is a piece of important reality. A home may have perfect appointments and impeccable care, but if the language used by the members reflects indifference, hostility, and selfishness, the chances are that much of the family living is not associated with loving.

Teenage Peter set up his tape recorder receiver in the centerpiece of the dining room table one day. As the family assembled for its evening meal together, Peter turned his equipment on to catch the family's table conversation. he did it as a prank to "bug" his parents. What the tape recorder caught was much, much more. When Peter played back the tape for the next family meeting, the results was sobering. He heard his own voice raised against his younger brother. Then little brother fussed about the food. His father's voice came loud and clear taking him to task for a chore he had neglected to complete. His mother complained of a headache and no one expressed sympathy or offered to help clear the table. Everyone sat silently as the replayed tape closed, until Peter said half under his breath, "Is that the way we really are?" His mother smiled in recognition of the situation and replied, "Every family has an off day now and then. Let's all try to make ours less frequent." "Amen to that," was Peter's response as he grinned sheepishly and left the room.

Changing pressures and tempos are to be expected in a family's emotional climate. Pressures build up at home when one or more members is under the strain of meeting personal obligations in community, church, school, or work. The tension of the anxious one infects the others, voices get edgy, and tempers are apt to be short. Then when success comes from a job well done, the mood of the family is one of relief and jubilation as they celebrate the victory together. Illness or worry upset a family almost without their being aware of why they are so peevish with one another. Then the sick one recovers, and the family's strength is renewed.

Every member of a family plays his or her part in setting the tone of family living. Everything may be going smoothly when one individual in the home disturbs its peace with an angry blast, a disgruntled complaint, or a moody cutting off of communication with the others. Some self-appointed peacemaker may step in with a bit of wit or an effort to smooth things out. If the uneasy one is mollified, the unpleasant moment passes quickly and the sun shines again in the family. All too often the unhappy mood of one member is caught by the others through one or more days when everything seems to go wrong.

Loving Is Shown in Many Ways

Love is expressed not only through hugs and kisses. It manifests itself in a myriad of ways within a family. Every family develops its own style of living and loving that is unlike that of any other home. What is right and good in one family would be artificial pretense in another. Thriving families grow more capable of loving as time goes by. Each loves in its own fashion that is clear to its members and may be less obvious to outsiders.

Openly affectionate families are easy to recognize. Members of expressive families kiss one another upon leaving or returning home. Father openly caresses and kisses his wife and children upon their coming together after a separation of any length. Mother holds out her arms to her husband and children for a welcoming embrace in the morning and a good night kiss at bedtime. The children are encouraged to express their affection freely for relative, close family friends, and members of the immediate family. Even the family pets are showered with love and endearments. What comes naturally to members of openly affectionate families is quite out of character for more formal, restrained persons who have learned a different language of loving in their homes.

LaVerne came from an exuberantly affectionate family where everyone kissed everyone else as a matter of course. Her Henry was a quiet nondemonstrative man, who rarely showed his feelings, even for those he loved. When LaVerne urged him to return her warm embraces, he became confused and embarrassed. It was not until LaVerne visited in Henry's home that she began to realize that Henry was doing what was natural for him. In time, Henry began to return her affection more visibly, and she in turn became somewhat more restrained in expressing her love. They each taught the other a new idiom of loving that added new dimensions to their relationship.

Quietly accepting families are warmed by a slow steady fire of affection. Their members are sure of their love for one another. They all are secure in being themselves because they know they are accepted for what they are without question. Such loving families encourage their members to tune into one another without question. Loving families encourage their members to tune into one another with receptive ears and hearts. They foster a quiet glow of fondness that is ever-present and unchanging.

Jesse came from such a family and as long as he lived he carried forth its precious heritage. His quiet warmth blessed every member of his large extended family who looked to him for loving compassion, regardless of what troubles they faced. His love for others drew people from all walks of life toward him with appreciation. As long as he lived he never was heard to speak harshly of another person. He loved everyone he knew with quiet acceptance. Now his children and grandchildren carry on his heritage in a way that is heartwarming. No one who ever knew him mistook his quiet undemonstrative way for indifference. One might not feel his touch, but his soul was in his eyes, and more was unnecessary.

Caring about through caring for go together. Loving is expressed through caring for another person. This is in both senses of the word—caring about what happens to him, and caring for him as a precious person of worth. This is beyond any sentimental expression of affection that is not backed up by genuine caring. When parents tell a teenager, "We love you so much that we let you do anything your heart desires," he may get the message, "We don't care what you do, live your own life and see if we care." Teenagers, too big for the cuddling and caressing they were given as little children, need to have their parents' love expressed in other ways. One of the most effective and usually the most greatly needed is in their parents ongoing, supportive caring both for and about them.

Teenagers feel secure in the tender loving care their parents give each other. When they observe frequent evidences that Mama loves Papa, they are reassured that all is well at home. Teenagers are sensitive to the ways in which a man cares for his wife both as his sweetheart and as a precious person to be protected and cherished. The mood of caring that parents demonstrate in their marriage is caught by their teenagers in ways that give them strength to mature and go on into homes of their own. Parental caring carries over in patterns of affection in the families their children establish. This is a precious heritage, more potent than many youngsters realize.

Parental Love Over the Years

"Love is what we have been through together," says a wise

pastor. In few relationships is this more true than those of parents and their children. Parents' loving care brings their baby through the difficult days of infancy and childhood. In the process of caring for a helpless baby and nurturing a little child, the parents grow ever more devoted to their charge; and the little one responds with the love of which he is capable. Accidents, illnesses, minor and major crises are met and overcome as parents and their child weather the first decade or more of life together. By the time the youngster reaches his teen years he is ready for a more grown-up kind of love for his parents that they wisely reciprocate in turn.

Cuddling comes naturally during childhood. As mother and father bathe or change a baby, they hold and fondle and caress him in ways that satisfy his need to be touched in loving ways. He returns their love in pats and hugs and peanut-butter kisses that warm their hearts. As he grows, he slips off their laps and ventures forth into the world of childhood. He hurts himself and comes running back to Mother to "kiss it and make it well." The little girl nestles into her father's lap and hears him tell her that she is his little sweetheart. She smooths her hair and smiles at him tenderly as she has seen her mother do. Even when she gets to be a big girl, she backs into him as he sits in his big chair, and asks him to "make a lap." She turns up her face to be kissed and returns her parents' love with her hugs and efforts to please. As time goes by she gets too big for the childish gestures of affection that once were so pleasant. Then she, her brother, and her parents enter a whole new phase of their relationship when new forms and expressions of loving must be developed.

How do porcupines love one another?" The answer is "very carefully." So it is with the show of affection between parents and teenagers. The boy who had been so affectionate as a little lad, now turns his back on his father's loving gestures. When his mother bends over his head to kiss him goodnight, he pulls the top of her robe together with an embarrassed grin, as he dodges her caress. He brushes off her good-bye kisses and begs her not to hug him in front of the guys. He plays it "real cool" as he struggles to attain manly ways.

The girl of the family who once was her daddy's little darling now but rarely comes close enough to kiss. She brushes off his advances in all except those rare intervals when she comes for comfort to his arms. Her mother hardly knows what is an acceptable demonstration of affection anymore. Most of the time her teenagers avoid her touch, and give her but a hasty peck on the cheek as a token of their regard. At other times, especially when she is alone with one of them, the old warmth shows through and they share a tender moment or two. Parents must learn a new language of loving as their children become teenagers. In time the young people become mature enough to trust themselves to again be openly demonstrative with their parents.

Calmer, quieter years lie ahead. As teenagers emerge into young adults, a new phase of relating to their parents begins. Once secure in their own independence, they are free to love and be loved with less fear of losing their autonomy. Now two generations of adults can relate to one another with mutual warmth. Mother and young adult daughter enjoy "girl-talk" as they work together on occasional projects. Their expressions of affection for one another come naturally out of the process of living and loving. Father warms to the touch of his son's arm thrown across his shoulder. The young man turns to his parents with questions he wants to discuss, problems he wants to solve, and triumphs he wants to share. The grown daughter of the family slips easily into and out of her parents' home once she is secure in a home of her own.

Welcoming Differences as Evidences of Love

Family members sometimes wonder why they can be so polite to strangers and so contentious at home. The answer is that they can afford to be courteous to strangers because they have little at stake with them. With family members their involvement is too deep to allow misunderstandings to go unexpressed. Differences matter among persons who are closely related. The more you love another person, the more easily he or she can hurt you. The closer you live with each other, the more often your differences become apparent. Loving one another heightens both the bright and the dark aspects of living together.

Different persons, ages, and ways are what makes family living an ever-present challenge. A family inevitably is made up of unique personalities each with his or her own qualities, strengths, and sense of selfhood. Though the members of a family share the same heritage, they each express it in their own way. Each person *has* to be different in order to avoid being but a hollow image of the others. Just as no two children in a family are exactly alike, so, too, no two members of any age in the home think, act, or feel like each other. This makes for a certain intensity of interaction that few nonfamily relationships share. It is because family members care about one another and feel unalterably bound to one another that magnifies their differences.

Varying styles add richness to family living. As teenagers stretch beyond their childish bonds to their parents, they explore new life-styles. Each develops his or her own talents that lead to new dimensions of experience for the young person and for those who love him. Rick is the son of a gentle and much-beloved minister of the gospel. He has been brought up to turn the other cheek and to harm no living creature. He now shows intense interest in healing sick animals and talks about going on into veterinary medicine as his lifework. His parents encourage this compassionate side of his nature at the same time that they are puzzled by his fascination with the manly art of self-defense. He has been in several karate exhibitions since he joined a "Y" class some time ago. Now he is quietly proud of his Black Belt which seems so out of character to those who know his gentle nature. His leader says that many a teenager joining his karate class finds a certain masculine pleasure in using his body expertly. This seems to be especially true of the slender, tender, considerate fellows who look for constructive ways of exerting their masculinity.

Sharing knowledge, attitudes, and values among different members of a family increases the life space of each. "I view the world through a dozen eyes," says an appreciative father of four. He goes on to say that he and his wife keep tuned to what their teenagers say because of all they value in what their youngsters are reporting. Today's teenagers know many things with which their parents are but vaguely familiar. The fields of electronics, of science, of space travel, of modern art, music, and sports are familiar to many a young person. Their reading and schooling have brought them understanding of things their parents never knew quite so intimately. Their feelings about themselves and the world around them color their attitudes in ways that are a revelation to their families. Their search for new forms of religious expression is stimulating to many a congregation. Their concern for the environment, for conservation, and for peace prick the conscience of their elders, and upon occasion they enlist their families in support of these causes. Meantime, more than they know they are enlarging, expanding, and enriching the values of their families inculcated over the years. Such shared lives are a boon to family, community, and nation.

Acceptance is the key to love in action. When a person feels that his family accepts him, no matter what he looks like, or what he does, he is free to be himself. Sally defines a family as a place where they love you even when you run around the house in your slip and wear your curlers until noon. Her brother, expresses himself more simply when he says more than anything else he appreciates his family's acceptance of his long hair and new beard. Some of the other fellows have been alienated from their parents by the family scenes over the way they look. He, in contrast, knows his family's acceptance in whatever hairstyle or clothing he adopts. Teenagers may be sloppy while they are busy trying on various life-styles while they can. Soon they will have to conform to what the adult world demands of its workers and its citizens. During the teen years acceptance by one's family of what one is and is trying to become is an expression of love.

The Grown-up Heart of the Family

Husband-wife love sets the tone for family living. Stronger than the mother-baby tie is the bond that binds man and wife into a single unity. Warmer than a father's love for his daughter is his feeling for his mate. More lasting than a mother's concern for her son is her caring for her spouse. Marital love is literally the heart of the home. It serves as the basis for the conception, birth, and nurturance of all of the children that arrive to bless the union. Then, long after the last child grows up and leaves home, husband and wife are warmed by their mutual love for one another, for as long as both shall live. This is the design of a marriage blessed by enduring devotion. Herein lies the tragedy of those couples whose union is broken somehow, somewhere along the way.

The single parent's double jeopardy lies in the absence of a mate, as well as in the lack of the second parent for the children. The mother, left alone for whatever reason, is husbandless, mateless, loverless, and partnerless in so very many ways. She finds herself a fifth wheel among couples in her social set. She has no mate with whom to confide the day's happenings. She lacks the emotional and sexual satisfactions once found with her husband. She does what she can to be both father and mother to her children, even when her efforts never seem quite adequate. The problem is no lighter for the father left to rear his children alone. He sorely misses his wife's homemaking, personal, social, and amorous services. He finds it impossible to replace a mother's care with help to rear the children. Relatives and friends do what they can to fill the vacuum left by the departed spouse, but the emptiness is still there at the heart of the home.

Down through the ages there have been families broken by the death of one of the parents. By the last quarter of the century, fewer homes were broken by death and more marriages were broken by divorce and separation. Many of these present-day break-ups might have been prevented if the partners had worked as hard preserving their marriages as they must do replacing them once they are dissolved.

Couple enrichment helps keep a marriage alive and thriving. Many hundreds of thousands of modern American couples each year enter into conscientious efforts to revitalize their marriages. Churches of the various denominations and religious faiths regularly offer retreats for married couples of their congregations. At the climax of some of these intense experiences in rediscovering one another, husbands and wives take again the vows of marriage and commit themselves anew to one another. Encounter groups under a variety of auspices are available in many communities for those who seek renewed awareness of themselves and others. Marriage counseling is an established profession devoted to the development and maintenance of vitally meaningful relationships. Mental health resources are available to treat emotionally ailing persons and relationships. These facilities are not only to prevent marital crackups. They serve best those couples who care enough about themselves and their families to keep functioning at their best.

Being good to live with is good marriage insurance. The husband who protects his health safeguards his family. The wife who satisfies her own deep needs as a person becomes a better mate and mother in her fulfillment. Being good to live with is much more than making an effort to adjust. At best, it is developing as a person to the place where one naturally does what is best for those one loves. It hardly helps his family for a man to drive himself to an early grave or to deprive them of his presence during their critical years. Similarly it is poor strategy for a mother to martyr herself for her children when other options are available for her. Modern-day Americans are encouraged to take care of themselves as well as one another in the family. To the extent to which they succeed, they keep alive and growing as persons with the capacity for making life good for themselves and those close to them.

Releasing their older children with loving trust is a prime task of parents as they ready themselves for the empty nest ahead. Mothers and fathers with confidence that they have reared their children well let them go forth into lives of their own as they become ready. This frees the young people of the sense of duty to their parents and the feeling of guilt at leaving their parents bereft when they leave. Quite as important is what releasing older teens and young adults does for the parents. Now, for the first time since they first married they are alone as a couple. Now, they can go and come as they will, without worrying about their young. Now, they can redecorate their home to suit themselves, without thought of what will best please and suit the children. Now, they can rediscover one another in the new burst of intimate communication to be found in the postparental years. Now they reap the rewards of parenthood in seeing their children go on to build lives of their own, while they discover the potentials of the decades of adulthood that remain for them.

Loving Is Caught from One Another

There is an infectious quality of love that is transforming. Anyone who loves another is himself radiantly aglow. As his love is returned, he is warmed again by its reflected glory. Each of us is susceptible to the experience of loving and being loved as long as we live. Each person catches and passes on love's blessing to every other person whose life he touches. This is particularly true in families where children early learn the meaning of loving in action. Indeed, this is the prime function of families—to demonstrate love's power in day-to-day living. Only thus may each new generation be grounded in security and lifted in love.

"I'm a better person when I'm with him," a teenage girl says of her first real sweetheart. She is discovering in this new relationship something her family taught her years ago—that love is patient and kind. Her father may question her choice of a boyfriend, but what she feels when she is with him is what her father introduced her to many years ago. Loving is transforming not only of the beloved, but of the lover as well. Each of us is a better person for having love in our lives. Each of us is at our best with those who love us for what we are. Herein lies the magic of loving in the family and beyond it, over the years.

"She believes in me," is potent power. Parents who see the swan in their ugly duckling generate the confidence the young teenager needs. Their belief in their young people inspire them to live up to their expectations. Their confidence in the goodness of life lights up the dark places in daily living, for themselves and for their teenagers. One of the saddest complaints a teenager can make is that his parents do not trust him. Happier by far are the young people who sense that their parents believe in them, enough to encourage them to go forth at their own pace, and in their own way. This is living and loving at its best.

Hold on to love—it is precious stuff! There is nothing silly or superficial about love. It is the most powerful force on earth. Without it the world would be a sorry place. Without it there would be no reason for families, or for fathers, or mothers, or children, or teenagers. Living is transformed by loving. Men and women, parents and children, families and communities all come into proper perspective with the lenses of loving. Love is too precious to keep to oneself. It grows as it is shared, and blesses as it is expressed. This is the triumph of parent and teenager, living and loving.